CAPSTONE

Smart

THINGS TO KNOW ABOUT

Brands &
Branding

JOHN MARIOTTI

INSTANT KNOWLEDGE

First published 1999 by
Capstone US   Capstone Publishing Limited
Business Books Network   Oxford Centre for Innovation
163 Central Avenue   Mill Street
Suite 2   Oxford OX2 0JX
Hopkins Professional Building   United Kingdom
Dover   http://www.capstone.co.uk
NH 03820
USA

British Library Cataloguing in Publication Data
A CIP catalogue record for this book is available from the British Library

ISBN 1-84112-039-1

Typeset by
Sparks Computer Solutions Ltd, Oxford
http://www.sparks.co.uk
Printed and bound by
T.J. International Ltd, Padstow, Cornwall

This book is printed on acid-free paper

Contents

What is Smart?

The *Smart* series is a new way of learning. *Smart* books will improve your understanding and performance in some of the critical areas you face today like *customers, strategy, change, e-commerce, brands, influencing skills, knowledge management, finance, teamworking, partnerships.*

Smart books summarize accumulated wisdom as well as providing original cutting-edge ideas and tools that will take you out of theory and into action.

The widely respected business guru Chris Argyris points out that even the most intelligent individuals can become ineffective in organizations. Why? Because we are so busy working that we fail to learn about ourselves. We stop reflecting on the changes around us. We get sucked into the patterns of behavior that have produced success for us in the past, not realizing that it may no longer be appropriate for us in the fast-approaching future.

There are three ways the *Smart* series helps prevent this happening to you:

- by increasing your self-awareness

- by developing your understanding, attitude and behavior

- by giving you the tools to challenge the status quo that exists in your organization.

Smart people need smart organizations. You could spend a third of your career hopping around in search of the Holy Grail, or you could begin to create your own smart organization around you today.

Finally a reminder that books don't change the world, people do. And although the *Smart* series offers you the brightest wisdom from the best practitioners and thinkers, these books throw the responsibility on you to *apply* what you're learning in your work.

Because the truly smart person knows that reading a book is the start of the process and not the end ...

As Eric Hoffer says, "In times of change, learners inherit the world, while the learned remain beautifully equipped to deal with a world that no longer exists."

David Firth
Smartmaster

Preface

In *Smart Things to Know about Brands & Branding* we will follow a progression of smart things to know. First comes the decision to create a brand and what the brand name is to be – a company name, a descriptive name or some kind of made-up name that means nothing until it is connected to whatever you want to spend the money to connect it with.

Next comes the understanding of what a brand means and why that is important. What the brand means – a shorthand way of expressing a complicated mixture of value and cachet – makes a big difference to what you can do with it.

That's why "what it means" is something we use specific terms to describe. "Brand character, brand identity, and brand image" are common terms that describe what the brand owner hopes consumers will think when they hear the brand name – or sometimes – what people do think, whether the owner of the brand likes it or not.

Once we have established what the brand's character, identity, and image are supposed to be (and hopefully are moving them in the right direction), another issue looms large. Who knows about the brand and who cares about it? How can a valuable brand be built and sustained over the long term?

First we must make the targeted customers aware of the brand. Then we must make it so desirable that we get them to prefer it and buy it. Finally we must make sure to deliver on the promise the brand makes, so that they will like it enough to buy it over and over and become loyal to the brand. Brand equity is the term coined to cover the combined value of awareness, loyalty, perception and associations. The value of a brand's equity can and often does exceed the value of all the other assets of a company.

If we have achieved these steps, we must learn about how to protect the brand from copycats, knock-off artists and robbers. This is a challenge in itself. If we can protect it, we sure better spend a lot of time and skill in managing it so that we make a lot of money on the products and services it is placed on. That is far from a sure thing. If we dilute, fragment, confuse or generally spoil the brand, we need some ideas on if and how it can be repaired, restored or rebuilt. Brands are like old houses – worthy of being fixed up unless they have weak foundations and are ready to collapse.

Last, we need to think about this whole new inter-networked, turbulent world in which everything is tumbled topsy-turvy into new piles. All of what we knew, that got us to where we are, is in danger of obsolescence. The rapidly accelerating, digital, information-based, computer and telecommunication-driven, globally, white-knuckle, gut wrenching (OK – you get the idea) revolution is changing everything – including some of the rules about brands and branding – but not all of them.

Introduction

The Importance and Value of Brands and Branding

HOW CAN THE CONFUSED CONSUMER DECIDE?

You go into a Wal*Mart or Carrefour superstore and you are faced with about 150,000 square feet (16,000 square meters) of product choices. The sheer expanse of choices is dizzying. The first challenge is to find the general area that has the kind of merchandise you are looking for. It is easy to wander aimlessly for 20–30 minutes and still not find what you wanted, even though you know it's in there somewhere. At other times, you find it and then wander off looking for something else, only to realize you don't know where the original area you found has gone. They didn't remove it from the store while you were shopping, but it seems like it at times. Then finally, *aha*! You found it – now the fun begins. Now the power of brands, branding, marketing, merchandising and promotion takes hold of your mind (and your wallet) like a wet sponge, and tries to wring out the desired behavior.

You say you need some small kitchen appliances? Perhaps a blender for those delightful tropical drinks in the summer, or a good coffee-maker, or better yet an automatic tea-brewer for the chilly months. As you enter the area occupied by categories like small electric appliances, a barrage of brand names in a wide array assaults your overloaded senses. Which is better? Is the Hamilton Beach a better blender than the cheaper Oster branded one next to it? Is the Braun or Procter-Silex coffeemaker better than the similarly priced Mr. Coffee is? How large a capacity teakettle do I need? I seldom drink 10–12 cups at a time! How on earth does a poor consumer decide what to buy out of all these options? The answer – they buy a brand they know and trust.

Want to do some housecleaning? No one likes this chore, but the average home accumulates 40 pounds of dust and dirt each year. Somehow it must be removed and disposed of. How about a vacuum cleaner? There are whole ranks of them. Panasonic, Bissell, Hoover, Eureka, and Dirt-Devil upright models stand on the display like silent soldiers, with their point of purchase materials crying for your attention. The canister models are over there; the handheld ones behind you. "Buy me", cries large print on the Dirt Devil, "I have MVP – maximum vacuum power." "No! Buy Me!" exclaims the Hoover, "I have wind-tunnel design for more efficient cleaning." The Eureka is cheaper than both, and looks a lot the same. The Bissell comes apart and is two cleaners in one. The Panasonic is high-tech

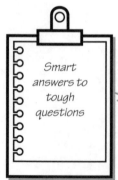

Smart answers to tough questions

Q: How on earth does a consumer decide what to buy?
A: When the prices are all about the same, consumers will buy what they have always bought – the brand that is most familiar and comfortable!

looking. What will you choose? Shopping for vacuum cleaners "sucks" says one confused consumer. But you will choose, and that choice will be heavily influenced by the brand name.

How about a simple pair of everyday blue jeans? The number of varieties is mind boggling. Faded denim, hard-denim, stonewashed denim, tapered, straight-leg, comfort-fit, relaxed-fit, classic fit are all modifiers you might find. Then there is the maker's brand to consider. Levi's, Lee, Wrangler, a house private-brand, and more face the discriminating consumer.

What size do you need? Well that depends on how honest you are. These are supposed to be comfortable, right. OK, buy the larger size – but wait – are these pre-shrunk? Pre-washed? Shrink-to-fit? Or are they just pre-washed and say nothing about shrinkage. As one saleswoman said, these are "shrink resistant." When I asked what that meant, she said, "they don't want to shrink, but they will!" Thanks a lot!

Smart things to say about brands

Brands have been important for a long time.

The choice will be made as much on what the tag that is left on the jeans has on it – the brand name – as on the color, fabric and size. Those are givens, but as they walk away from the guys, the girls want the Levi's red tab or the Lee fitted jeans to be noticed. The favored brand will be the choice for her *derrière* decoration.

Do you get the idea by now? A universe of choice faces consumers, and the only help they can find is the brand name they heard about, know about, or bought, trusted and enjoyed the last time. Strong, familiar, recognizable and trusted brand names will win the struggle for the consumer's money, unless their owners do stupid things and confuse, mis-use or spoil the brand.

Procter & Gamble, one of the world's brand leaders, used brands this way almost half a century ago when people went to their grocery stores with lists of the brands (not commodities) they wanted. Shoppers usually spoke with the proprietor/owner of the store, and the brands had to be easy to remember, easy to pronounce, and not likely to be misinterpreted. Often grocers would take orders via telephone and deliver the groceries – a phenomenon that is being resurrected with the Internet replacing the telephone. "What goes around comes around" in many more ways than we realize.

A retired Procter & Gamble marketing executive

Branding grew up around the turn of the last century to do the same thing in many respects as it is doing today – provide the consumer with a shorthand name for a known and/or preferred package of quality and consistency.

Time is a perishable commodity, and none of us has enough of it. As if that isn't enough of a problem, there is more information available now than ever. The explosion of information and products confuses time-starved consumers with too many choices and too little time to choose. Helping to choose is exactly what brands and branding can do for your product or service, unless poor brand management weakens the brand, or poor company management weakens the company that owns the brand.

Smart things to say about brands

A recognized and trusted brand name provides the only practical way to simplify the purchase decisions for consumers.

Coke's globally recognized brand name is worth tens of billions of dollars. In 1998, Coke plowed $900 million into marketing support for its largest bottler, Coca-Cola Enterprises. Coke spent $115 million in just US advertising in 1998 to support its flagship brand. Intel created a premium priced, highly profitable brand from a once anonymous component – the PC microprocessor. What computer should you buy? The one with Intel Inside, of course. Lexus has become synonymous with luxury automobiles in less than a decade.

As recently as 1994 – only about 5 years ago, no one had ever heard of Yahoo!, amazon.com, or eBay. Now Yahoo!, amazon.com, and eBay stocks all sell at huge multiples to the highest imaginable estimates of their earnings – if they have any earnings at all. Their "brands" are the names of the companies' Internet sites. Consumers, who recognize these brands, not only use them on the Internet, but also buy their stocks, bidding prices to astronomical levels. Brand power is immense!

Rubbermaid, one of the US's best known, most admired brands was sold recently to Newell, who owns a stable of recognizable consumer brands like Mirro cookware, Levelor blinds, Sanford and Eberhard-Faber writing instruments, and dozens more. The remarkable part of this transaction was that Rubbermaid stock was languishing in the low to mid-$20s and Newell offered a stock swap worth almost $40 per share. According to analysts, the entire premium – almost double the market price – was due to the value of Rubbermaid's brand name. Clearly, the Newell-Rubbermaid merger proves that brand names are valuable. If brands are so valuable, there must be some "smart things to know" about brands and branding.

Smart quotes

A powerful brand frequently provides the source of a company's wealth for many generations. The best brands improve with age, developing clearly defined personalities, as well as the affection and loyalty of the public. The best become parents to sub-brands and brand extensions, which give the owner a chance to exploit their values and names in new areas.

Interbrand Group PLC, *The World's Greatest Brands* (New York University Press, 1997)

INTERBRAND: THE WORLD'S GREATEST BRANDS

The World's Greatest Brands ranks the top 100 global brands, and separates out the top 10 brands in 15 industry sectors, including fashion and luxury goods, automotive and oil, food, financial services, technology, retail and media, among others. In determining the world's top 100 brands, Interbrand assessed more than 350 brands according to four criteria:

- *brand weight*: influence or dominance over competitors in the market (e.g. McDonald's dominance in the quick-service restaurant industry);
- *brand length*: successful extension into other markets (e.g. Virgin's development into airline, soft drinks and radio);
- *brand breadth*: across age, religion and nationality (e.g. Coca Cola's worldwide appeal);
- *brand depth*: customer commitment (i.e., loyalty to The Body Shop for their environmental values).

1. McDonald's	19. BMW
2. Coca Cola	20. American Express
3. Disney	21. Tampax
4. Kodak	22. Nintendo
5. Sony	23. Lego
6. Gillette	24. Ikea
7. Mercedes -Benz	25. Sega
8. Levi's	26. Harley-Davidson
9. Microsoft	27. Intel
10. Marlboro	28. Body Shop
11. IBM	29. KFC
12. Nike	30. Heinz
13. Johnson & Johnson	31. Toyota
14. Visa	32. Xerox
15. Nescafé	33. CNN
16. Kellogg's	34. Adidas
17. Pepsi-Cola	35. Pillsbury
18. Apple Computer	36. Reebok

37. Cadbury's	69. Fuji
38. Camel	70. Duracell
39. Chanel	71. BP
40. Swatch	72. Johnnie Walker
41. Harrods	73. Polaroid
42. Colgate	74. Louis Vuitton
43. Toshiba	75. Volvo
44. Mars	76. Hewlett-Packard
45. Ford	77. Boeing
46. Time	78. Zippo
47. Barbie	79. Casio
48. Rolex	80. Volkswagen
49. Lucky Strike	81. Ray-Ban
50. BBC	82. Smirnoff
51. British Airways	83. Budweiser
52. MasterCard	84. Philips
53. Mitsukoshi	85. Sears
54. FedEx	86. Pampers
55. AT&T	87. Schweppes
56. Persil	88. Nivea
57. Heineken	89. Reader's Digest
58. Campbells	90. Kleenex
59. Fisher-Price	91. Canon
60. Marks & Spencer	92. Virgin
61. Motorola	93. The Financial Times
62. Porsche	94. Haagen-Dazs
63. Reuters	95. Braun
64. Shell	96. Samsung
65. Mattel	97. Gordons
66. Honda	98. Benetton
67. Pizza Hut	99. Sainsbury
68. Compaq	100. Dr. Martens

The World's Greatest Brands (New York University Press, New York, NY). Interbrand, 437 Madison Avenue, New York, NY. Website: www.interbrand.com

Losing control of a brand can be a serious problem when companies expand globally. When I was head of Huffy Bicycles, we spent millions to elevate our brand to the best known US bicycle brand while Schwinn, the former brand leader, struggled to survive as a company, and lost focus on their brand. When we began to sell Huffy Bicycles to Toys 'R Us around the world, Huffy was forced to buy back the trademark for its brand name in Spain. Local entrepreneurs had registered Spanish trademarks for many leading US consumer product names, including Huffy and Nike, and then sold the rights back to the original owners at hugely inflated prices. Because brands carry with them an implied promise of a certain mixture of value, the owners of these brands must be careful to stay in control so they can assure that the promise of the brand's value is not broken.

Hewlett-Packard announced their intention to sell their products under another brand name, Apollo, for the first time. They plan to use this "subbrand" on ink-jet printers retailing for under $100 and do not want to discount the prestigious HP brand to such low retail priced products. HP also launched a new $150 million series of ads designed to position this large powerful company's brand name as a force on the Internet. Rivals IBM and Sun Microsystems have already done this positioning with great success. There is no doubt that strong brands and the power and reach of the Internet together make for a powerful partnership.

KILLER
QUESTIONS

What does a smart brand leader have to watch out for?
- If we don't protect our brand using every legal device available, might we lose control of it?
- How can we be sure the brand always delivers on its value the promise?
- Can we make sure that no one takes the importance of this protection too lightly?

- Richard Reizenstein, PhD, professor of Marketing and acting Dept. Head, *Marketing Logistics & Transportation*, University of Tennessee-Knoxville, College of Business Administration.

- Roger Blackwell, PhD, professor of Marketing and Consumer Behavior at Ohio State University, and leading consultant on retailing; author of the widely used textbook, *Consumer Behavior* and of several other books, including *From the Edge of the World* (Ohio State University Press) and most recently *From Mind to Market* (Harper Business 1997).

- David Aaker, PhD, professor of Marketing, Haas School of Business, University of California at Berkeley and author of the books *Managing Brand Equity* and *Building Strong Brands* (Free Press 1994, 1996).

- Bernd Schmitt and Alex Simonson, professors and authors of *Marketing Aesthetics: The Strategic Management of Brands, Identity, and Image* (Free Press 1997).

- Tom Duncan & Sandra Moriarity, professors at the University of Colorado, former advertising and public relations executives and authors of *Driving Brand Value* (McGraw-Hill 1997).

- Regis McKenna, Chairman, The McKenna Group, Palo Alto, CA. consultant to numerous start-up companies, and author of *Real Time* and *Relationship Marketing* (Harvard Business School Press 1997, 1991).

- Jack Trout, author of several books including *Positioning – The Battle for your Mind*, (McGraw Hill 1981) and *The New Positioning* (McGraw Hill 1996), a consultant to major corporations.

- Al Ries & Laura Ries authors of several books including *Positioning – The Battle for your Mind* (McGraw Hill 1981) and *22 Immutable Laws of Branding*, and consultants in marketing strategy to major corporations.

- Joe Marconi, President, S&S Public Relations, former advertising executive with Weber, Cohn & Reilly, and author of *Crisis Marketing* (Probus 1992), *Getting the Best from your Ad Agency* (Probus 1991) and *Beyond Branding – How Savvy Marketers Build Brand Equity to Create Products and Open New Markets* (Probus 1993).

SMART PEOPLE
TO HAVE ON
YOUR SIDE

Almost six out of ten consumers agree, "I don't have time to investigate the quality of different brands – I just buy the same brand I bought last time."

Kevin Clancy & Robert Shulman, *Marketing Myths that are Killing Business* (McGraw-Hill 1994)

Want to buy a new car made with just a few used parts – or how about a new computer with just a few used parts? Packard-Bell computers lost precious distribution and tarnished their image a few years ago when they were discovered to be using "recycled" (that is a nice word for used and returned) components in computers that were portrayed as "new." Whether the computer actually was lessened in utility value by this fact is irrelevant. The consumer's perception of the product brand was lessened and this perception is the consumer's reality until it is changed by some other factor. Compaq, IBM, Toshiba and many others jumped into the space lost by Packard-Bell and their well-known brand names permitted them to hold onto it even now – 3 years later!

Habits are very powerful, and in the absence of time, the established habits take over. When a brand becomes the consumers' preferred choice, they become very loyal to buying/using that brand of product or service. This

Q: Are brands and habits related, and are they valuable?
A: You bet they are! Habits are very powerful, and in the absence of time for new decisions, the established habits take over. When a brand becomes the consumers' preferred choice, they become very loyal to habitually buying/using that brand of product or service. This habit of consumer brand loyalty is what makes brands worth billions of dollars.

consumer brand loyalty is what makes brands worth millions or billions of dollars (or Euros).

Thanks to Interbrand, a leading global brand development company, there is a published ranking of the World's Greatest Brands. As you read more of *Smart Things to Know About Brands and Branding*, you will be able to form your own views about these and many other brands – and whether you agree with their criteria and assessments. It is interesting to note that at least two of the highest-rated brands, and possibly several more, are struggling financially as this is being written – perhaps for losing sight of how to maintain their brand: Kodak and Levi's are disappointing Wall Street. McDonald's, Disney, Kellogg's and Coke are not enjoying the stock values their brands seem to merit. All of these leading brand companies have made major changes over the past year or two in hopes of protecting their valuable brand franchise.

Smart quotes

… everything we thought we knew is wrong now, or will no longer apply.

Peter Drucker.

Anything worth that kind of warm-up is worthy of learning more about – so let's get on with *Smart Things to Know about Brands & Branding*. After all, the world has changed just while you've been reading this – so hurry up or you (and it) will be obsolete before you finish.

1

The Brand

WHAT IS A BRAND, ANYWAY?

A *brand* is a simplified "shorthand" description of a package of value upon which consumers and prospective purchasers can rely to be consistently the same (or better) over long periods of time. It distinguishes a product or service from competitive offerings. The influence of the Internet, e-commerce and globalization on brands will be profound.

What is a brand? The definition of brand

What a silly question. Everybody knows what a brand is – don't they? The answer, like the tag line for a recent Hertz's ad campaign is "not exactly!"

Oh, so you think this is simple. Well, give me a little time, a handful of professors to quote and I'll have you so confused you'll cry "uncle," and

A brand is a trusted promise of quality, service and value, established over time and proven by the test of repeated use and satisfaction.

let me explain it to you properly. Give up? Good, then let's get on with it.

Here's a serious long definition. A brand or brand name, as some people call it, is a simplified, "shorthand" description of a package of value upon which consumers and prospective purchasers can rely to be consistently the same (or better) over long periods of time. It distinguishes a product or service from competitive offerings.

However we choose to define it, a brand is an important asset of a company, its products or services and its marketing strategy. Often the brand will have a familiar logo associated with it as its icon. When you see this logo (such as the Nike swoosh), you think of the brand and the entire package of value and promises it carries. At least that is the way it is supposed to work!

Smart quotes

A brand is the proprietary visual, emotional, rational and cultural image that you associate with a company or a product.

Charles R. Pettis III
(Brand Solutions)

History of branding: where brands came from

I know – you always hated history in school – but to know where you are and where you might be going, it helps to know where you came from! Stick with me on this part, and you'll see how it all fits.

Branding formally came into widespread use only in the past century, but "brands" based on the reputations of craftsmen have existed over the centuries. Artisans usually marked their work with a symbol that was their unique brand. Later, ranchers in the old west used brands to identify their cattle. Since there were no fences until barbed wire was invented, this was the only way to mark their valuable property. As retailing grew and spread,

What is a brand? A brand is just a word: Kleenex, Xerox, or Jell-O. It is the core of your strategy, your DNA. It embodies your image, determines your marketing from concept to execution, includes assets and liabilities, and influences internal and external customers … Beauty is in the eye of the beholder. Your brand is who you are.

David R. Rohlander, "Positioning for the Future" in *Executive Excellence*, March 1999

brands became the manufacturer's way of marking their goods with a symbol of their reputation.

In post World War II, the consuming public was hungry for goods that had been unavailable due to resources devoted to the war efforts. An entire generation was scrambling to create new lives that were stable and secure – after all, that was why they had been fighting the war! Part of this security was the ability to have families and provide homes for them with amenities and comforts that the previous wars and the (US) depression had denied them.

KILLER QUESTIONS

What is a brand, anyway?

This era was wonderful for manufacturers. They could seldom make enough for the hungry consumers' desires. Many of today's great brands grew up in this era, as did the strategies and knowledge about brand management. The famous AIDA model arose from this post-war era. First, build **A**wareness of a brand, then create or find consumer **I**nterest in the brand. Next, build a **D**esire to purchase the brand to fulfill some real or imagined need, and finally incite the consumer to take **A**ction – go buy the brand.

What is the single most important objective of the marketing process? ...
We believe it's the process of branding. Marketing is building a brand in
the mind of the prospect. If you can build a powerful brand, you will have
a powerful marketing program. If you can't then all the advertising, fancy
packaging, sales promotion, and public relations in the world won't help
you achieve your objective.

Al Ries and Laura Ries, "World Class Brands" in *Executive Excellence*,
March 1999

Marketers discovered that awareness also had another powerful by-product – it led to loyalty, but only after trial purchases, and then repeat purchases. This AIDA model was the paradigm of choice for decades – until the world changed so radically that it was no longer sufficient.

Thus came the four "P"s: Product, Price, Promotion, and Place. Combine these in the right mixture and brand success was yours. This approach worked so well, that it withstood the test of time for decades. Once again, this model is not wrong *per se*, just not sufficient for a new era of marketing and branding. Once you know this, you can build on it.

As decades passed, wants and needs of the post-war era were fulfilled, and demand moderated. New products began to fail in record numbers. "Good enough" was no longer good enough. Twenty-five years ago the new product failure rate was 65%. Today it is 95%! This happened in spite of all of the accumulated brand knowledge and marketing expertise. Generics came to life, as did private labels and store brands. Brand loyalty for major brands was being undermined.

Margins for once-great brands kept shrinking, starving their advertising budgets. The price premium for many major brands has been disappearing in many instances. Only the most astute brand management can now hang onto a price premium. Will that be you and your company? The world has changed. Competition has changed. Because of this, brand management must also change. The old model is not wrong – it just isn't enough! You are on the threshold of a great era of opportunity – if you are willing to learn and then act on that learning. With this historical background, let's return to what a brand is and where it comes from.

The three ages of brands

The first age
A brand functions solely to differentiate a product and less often a service from its direct competitors. This is like the early ranchers' use of branding, when brands on cattle meant nothing more than who owned the cattle. Wells-Fargo was the brand of the stage-coach service.

- *Objective: Capture as large a share of consumers' wallets as possible.*

The second age

The brand starts to detach from and overshadow products and services it represents. Advertising becomes a powerful force. Line extensions abound. Consumers buy brands for status value and identity. (Nike, Harley-Davidson, Polo) Consumers become more fickle and less loyal. Brands become highly valued assets of companies (Coke, Marlboro).

- *Objective: Capture as large a share of consumers' minds as possible.*

The third age

Brands become increasingly autonomous, providing a device by which corporations are shaping the very ideology of the world! Millennial brands begin to evolve, underpinned by an amalgam of information, entertainment, experiences, images, and feelings. (Intel, Disney) Advertising grows in volume and importance: $39 billion worldwide in 1950; $256 billion worldwide in 1990.

- *Objective: Capture the largest possible share of consumers' lives, and even their souls!*

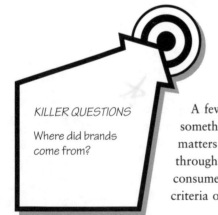

KILLER QUESTIONS

Where did brands come from?

How brand names are chosen – and why

Brand names come from all kinds of places.

A few people in a back room somewhere say "let's just make something up – it doesn't matter." Wrong! It does matter, and it matters more than ever these days with more brands competing through more media channels for less time and attention span of consumers. It matters a lot! Smart brand builders will recall the criteria of the old days – easy to remember, easy to spell and pronounce, hard to be confused with competing products, and so forth – not a bad place to start.

Of course, some of the original brands were the names of company founders – Sear, Roebuck & Co., and Ford Motor Company are two famous ones. That will always be the case, but those brands were built over many decades. Who has that much time, patience, and cash flow these days? A brand is sometimes the corporate name of the company who provides the product or service – like Intel or America Online. But these were launched and built at great effort and expense! If I get one more of those America Online disks in the mail, I'll scream. They come in magazines, with newspapers, or with junk mail; why, I even expect to find them in the toilets at airports (haven't yet though)! But, it worked! Persistence and numerous, frequent impressions build awareness, and as you'll see later, few things are more valuable than a brand with strong awareness.

At other times the brand is a descriptive name, which carries some strong connotations about what the product will do – like Pampers or Huggies disposable diapers, or High Endurance deodorant, but never mentions the corporate parent company. These kinds of brands are very effective because their name conveys useful information before you know anything else about them.

> The brand starts as a product and a name, but much can be built on that name. In fact, a brand name can be best described as the foundation stone for an elaborate edifice … Branding shapes a wealth of perceptions, beliefs, attitudes, and experiences to turn a product and name into something to which the consumer relates.
>
> *The World's Greatest Brands*

SMART VOICES

Professional brand builders use concept testing and focus groups to zero in on desirable brand names. If you are smart, you will too! These are time-proven approaches to sorting out what consumers prefer and what images the various names create in their mind.

In still other cases, the brand is a carefully invented name upon which the product or service value and image is conferred by advertising or promotion – like Lucent Technologies, Procter & Gamble's Tide and Cheer detergents, and Japanese luxury automobiles Lexus and Acura. Korean auto maker Hyundai should have made up a new name, because no one knew how to say Hyundai, and even fewer knew it was a car (it wasn't – it was a company name).

At other times, the aroma, the feel, the technology or some other characteristic of the product or service is implied in the name, like Xerox copiers, Soft-Scrub cleaner, Old Spice after-shave or Speedy delivery service. Services can also become brand names. Certainly American Express or FedEx are well known service brand names; so are package delivery company UPS and eSchwab, the electronic stock brokerage. If you are quick and aggressive, you can now grab good brand names and register them (and the domain names on the web that go with them) even without more than a few samples (that you sell in interstate commerce) of a product or service to use them on. That is how important names can be tied up for future use.

Brand names also do a couple of other things for you – when/if they are well chosen and properly positioned. Brands can help your product or service relate to the prospective buyer's sense of self-concept. People will buy things that they feel reinforces who they are or want to be. Brands also serve as the identification link between the shelf package and the actual product. This might be via an icon like a logo. It might be via a distinctive graphic look. Kodak film's yellow box, which along with Owens-Corning's pink fiberglass insulation are instances of colors being so distinctive an identification of a brand that they were allowed to be trade-marked. That is your job to do.

Some brands are actually "licenses" of either characters or themes from major movie and TV entertainment events like Star Wars, or the Muppets (from PBS TV's Sesame Street). Any one of the many Disney hit movies like *The Lion King* or even live action entertainment like WWF wrestling or NBA professional basketball, PGA golf, etc can create marketable brand names. Do the names Simba, Michael Jordan and Tiger Woods sound familiar? Yes, even mythical characters and real people can become brand names in their own way. Seinfeld is a brand name. TV shows become brand names. *Baywatch* – the world's most widely watched TV show is a brand name now. Recording artists become brand names! Celine Dion is a big brand name right now. So are the Backstreet Boys and the Spice Girls.

Times change, and popular celebrities and events change, and their brands come and go with them. Timing is everything in using such popular but

Q: If there are so many ways to create brand names, why can't anybody just pick a name and make it a successful brand name?

A: There are many reasons that this is not as easy as it sounds, but the most common ones are:

- the best names are already taken and registered or in use.
- choosing a new name is more difficult than it seems and is a kind of a science in itself.
- creating recognition for a name is very expensive and takes time.
- supporting the name with a product or service that delivers on the promise the name makes is harder than it seems – often much harder.

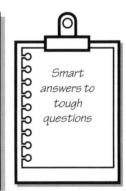

Smart answers to tough questions

trendy brands. If you wonder what to do in these crazy, fast-moving times you are not alone. Everyone wonders the same thing. As you read through this book, and form decisions, analyze them quickly and make them fast, or someone else will beat you to the market.

The global reach of brands

All brands are not globally equal

The greatest brands are those that are globally known and desired. It is very important for smart brand builders to understand the meaning, reach and (global) familiarity of the brand name when considering its power and value. Many brands are known the world over – Microsoft Windows, Coke, Levi's, Pepsi, Nike, Sony, IBM, Gucci, Mercedes-Benz, Polo/Ralph Lauren, Chanel, Rolls-Royce, McDonald's, and many, many more. Other brands are very popular locally or regionally in specific markets, but have widely varying brand recognition and appeal elsewhere the world: Rubbermaid (housewares) in North America, Cadbury (chocolates) in UK, Fiat (autos) in Europe, Renault and Peugeot (autos) in France, Carrefour (retailing) in Europe, CIFRA (retailing) in Mexico, Asahi (beer) in Japan, and many others.

These kinds of examples are countless, and you can find in any country or region. When I was president of Huffy Bicycles, we studied Europe and found that each major country had its own "famous" bicycle brand(s): Raleigh in England, B-H in Spain, Peugeot and Gitane in France, Kettler and Kynast in Germany, Bianchi in Italy. Of these, only Raleigh had a truly global presence. No-one had created a Pan-European bicycle brand. There were lots of reasons why. Most of them had to do with tradition and cultural preferences, but as cable TV spans Europe and the Euro be-

> In the consumer's mind, there is no difference between a company or product name and a brand name … From a business point of view, branding in the marketplace is very similar to branding on the ranch. Create in the mind of the prospect the perception that there is no product on the market quite like yours.
>
> Al Ries and Laura Ries, "World Class Brands" in *Executive Excellence*, March 1999

comes the currency – why not a single bike brand available in all the major countries. No one has yet pursued that idea up through the 1990s, but it is still an intriguing concept.

Another instance is that of Coca Cola, which uses the Fanta brand for fruit flavored soft drinks on an extensive global basis, but on a limited scale in their home US, where they are attempting to transfer that fruity image to Minute-Maid brand (although not too successfully at this time!).

Beware of "no-name" brands

It is worth a minute to discuss what brands are not. Simply because a company name is essentially its brand name, this does not mean it conveys any useful or positive image of the company, its products or services. When the company name fails to do that, it fails one of the primary tests of a brand name. What does EG&G stand for? How about USI, or USF&G? Chances are, you don't know – and the odds are you don't care! What about VF? Ring any bells? Did you know it is the largest producer and marketer of jeans in the US mass retail market? Not likely! If I had said Wrangler or Lee jeans, you might have reacted right away – those are two of VF's brand names. *House and Garden Magazine* very un-cleverly changed its name and brand logo to HG, and essentially destroyed what was a well-known magazine brand. It is being rejuvenated now. How? By re-naming it … *House & Garden*! Amazing? Yes. Surprising? No!

Company names can be different from their brand names

Companies often choose to remain behind the scenes and let their individual brands stand for what each best signifies – such as Newell Corporation who has a stable of dozens of well-known house-wares and hardware brands – but as a company is practically anonymous with consumers. Procter & Gamble is far from anonymous, but historically they have carefully avoided mixing their brand names with their corporate name. Only now, as they move into certain foreign markets are they associating the P&G identity with products – because it is the most recognizable name they have in those markets – and conveys an image of trusted value. Mars candies uses individual product names like M&Ms, Milky Way, Snickers, Mars, etc., whereas competitor Hershey uses its corporate name on more products, although no longer as exclusively as was once the case.

When brands are very well known and respected, and have dominant market positions, they can almost become household words: Xerox, Kleenex, Formica, and Scotch tape. This can be good news for the brand owner, but requires careful management, since too much of this kind of "good thing" can put the brand's trademark protection at risk. This topic will be discussed later when we deal with protecting brands.

KILLER QUESTIONS

What purpose do brands serve?

Before we close this chapter, let's review. Brands are symbolic. They are proprietary. They convey a message and a promise about value. At times a single symbolic icon conveys the brand. The size of the company is no factor in creating or owning a brand, but the amount of resources that can be applied in designing, selecting, promoting and supporting one makes a lot of difference.

The memorability of the brand is best when it is descriptive of what the product does or of a key benefit of the product or service. Company names are good brand names only if the company (or products and services) have

Q: What are the some of the most common reasons people buy brands?
A: Top five reasons to buy a brand:
1. Quality
2. Durability
3. Recognition
4. Trust
5. Acceptance by user

From Leo J. Shapiro & associates, a survey on licensed products and brands sold predominantly to children, Discount Store News, 1998

Smart answers to tough questions

been globally prominent for a long time as the premier provider of such things – like IBM and American Express for example.

The Internet/world-wide-web changes the rules

A new phenomenon has burst onto the brands and branding scene in the past five years – the Internet/world-wide-web. The explosive growth of this new, rapidly responding, all-pervasive form of media is changing many of the rules of brands and branding that were developed over decades. Now anyone with access to a computer and an Internet connection can create a web site and begin launching a brand. The up-front investment is almost zero.

It is little wonder that the most dramatic pricing move on the Internet is to give things away free – a price of zero. The smart manager in the Internet age realizes that everything is now changing and faster than ever. This means brands and their creation, usage and promotion must be continuously reviewed in the light of the most recent changes. The brand needs to be a stable foundation but not an anchor to old, outdated ways.

Costs that traditionally were proportional to transactions are now negligible. Brands have sprung up like weeds after a spring rain. Companies like Yahoo!, eBay, priceline, @Home, broadcast.com and millions of oth-

Smart quotes

Differentiation will then be more and more laid at the door of branding rather than product development with the result that the ratio of marketing to manufacturing costs will further diverge.

Hazel Kahan (Partner, Hazel Kahan Research), "Brand Survival In Millennial Times" ARF 43rd Conference. NYC, April 1997

ers have existed for less time than traditional companies took to get going, yet are rapidly becoming household "brands" with all the associated recognition and value. Perhaps this is why these companies' stocks trade at what were previously considered insane multiples to their sales and their earnings (if there are any earnings!).

Conclusions – mega-millennial brands

The evolution of brands has led us to a Millennial Brand position. In this Millennial Brand era, the brand has separated from products and the advertising is now separating from the design, manufacturing, distribution and sale of the products. I will use the example of Nike shoes, but I could use many other products or services interchangeably in this description.

SMART VOICES

RATING THE STRENGTH OF BRANDS

Four factors are considered good indicators of the strength of a brand – how dominant it is against competitors, how strong it is for brand extension, how long it has existed/how broad its awareness is, and how committed its buyers are to it:

- *brand weight:* influence or dominance over competitors in the market (e.g. McDonald's dominance in the quick-service restaurant industry)
- *brand length:* successful extension into other markets (e.g. Virgin's development into airline, soft drinks and radio)
- *brand breadth:* across age, religion and nationality (e.g. Coca Cola's worldwide appeal)
- *brand depth:* customer commitment (e.g. loyalty to The Body Shop for their environmental values).

Interbrand, *World's Greatest Brands*

The visual and functional design of Nike shoes is an important element of how the brand is positioned and presented, but who makes the shoes is almost irrelevant. The name of the particular shoe model is important, but how they are distributed is taken for granted. Who sells them, or how they are sold (unless it is in a Nike-Town store) is neutered. That they are Nike shoes is what matters. That they exist to say something to and about the wearer is what matters. The power of the brand is what it means to the purchaser – not as something to wear on the feet, but as a statement about what they mean to purchasers' ego, self-image, lifestyle, and emotions. This is what mega-Millennial Brands have become all about.

Throughout this book, I will revisit some of the implications of the Internet and world-wide-web on brands and branding. A Smart Thing to Know about brands and branding would not be complete without consideration of where this is all heading. The entire final chapter will consider this issue. Now let's get on with more Smart Things to Know about Brands and Branding.

2

Brand Origin and Image

WHERE DO BRANDS COME FROM, AND WHAT ARE
BRAND EQUITY, BRAND IMAGE *AND*
BRAND CHARACTER *ALL ABOUT?*

Companies create brands, on purpose or accidentally. Many brands are just the names of the founders or a slang name for the product, while others are carefully "engineered" and built.

Now that you are an expert on what a brand is and where they come from, remember that group of people who were just going to make up a name and go with it? Well, if they did, don't lend them any money – they are likely out of business by now. Playing the lottery or betting on a single number in roulette has big payoffs, but terrible odds. In business, the big payoffs make the news, but for every one of them, there are a hundred, a thousand, maybe a hundred thousand who lose – and go broke. A few

may cling to a meager existence, but never achieve real
success. Choosing brand names the right way is very
important.

Repeat after me: "Choosing brand names the right way
is very important." Again: "Choosing brand names the
right way is very important." Having drilled that point
in to your mind, lets move on!

In this chapter, we will explore where brands come from,
and what's meant by the familiar terms *brand strategy*,
brand equity, and *brand image* and *brand character*.
These are important aspects of creating and managing a
brand for maximum strategic success.

It used to be that brands were just for the big companies – those with
mega-buck advertising budgets and corporate communications departments. Not anymore. *Fast Company* magazine featured a cover issue last
year entitled "Brand YOU." The message is simple – brands are for small
and large businesses and all of those in-between, including individuals.
The small brands may not have the same kind of clout,
reach or appeal as the large ones, but may be no less
important in their segment of the market whether that is
a micro-niche, and small city or a faithful following on
the Internet.

Companies of all kinds and sizes create brands, usually
on purpose but sometimes accidentally. Many brands are
just the names of the founders, like Ben & Jerry's, or
Joe's Garage. Some are an intended slang name for the
product, like Levi's Dockers, or for a search engine like
"infoseek." Others are carefully "engineered" like Lexus,

Acura, and Lucent Technologies, which I will discuss in more detail later. Some are the company name, like General Electric, Microsoft, or Intel. Still others are sub-brands for a product like Microsoft "Windows" or the "children" of a large parent like Procter & Gamble (Tide, Bounty, Charmin, and dozens of others) or Newell-Rubbermaid Corporation (Mirro, Farberware, Levelor, Sanford, Eldon and many more).

Brand names can come from just about anywhere! Some are even the names of the founder's pets like Old Roy, the world's best-selling dog food, sold at Wal*Mart, and named after Sam Walton's hunting dog. Chevrolet was the name of a French race-car driver, Mercedes was the name of the daughter of the company's Paris sales representative, and Edsel – the notorious US auto failure of several decades ago – that was the name of one of Henry Ford's sons.

Smart things to say about brands

Choosing brand names the right way is very important.

My father was a professional musician with his own band in the early part of the US big band era, and he was nicknamed "Hinky" after the series of nights when his band played the 1920's hit tune *Hinky, Dinky, Parlez Vous*. It was so unusual as a nickname, it stuck as a theme, and his band was known forever after as "Hinky's Royal Commanders" – its brand name! Wherever these brands come from, a few points about them are critical – the brand strategy, its image/identity, and its character, position and personality.

Brand Strategy

Match brand strategy and product strengths to succeed

One expert on strategy holds that a superior strategy is a different strategy, and this view is a good one. That is a good starting place for a strategy when relating it to a brand. Differentiation is one of the key elements, and many people think the most important aspect of brands and branding.

The integration of the strategy with the creation, selection and differentiation of a brand and the development of products or services is essential. If you don't develop a strategy first or at least concurrently with the brand, there is a great risk that the brand development will be unsuccessful. If the brand does not fit the strategy and vice-versa, the results will not be very good, and may be terrible. If the brand strategy is not different from (or better than) what is already out there, creating demand for the brand will be difficult or impossible

A good example of this is Japanese automaker Subaru, who tried for years, unsuccessfully, to go head-to-head against larger, stronger, and better-financed rivals Toyota, Honda and Nissan. Only when Subaru chose a different niche strategy based on their 4-Wheel Drive technology and uniquely compatible horizontal engine were they able to compete with these larger stronger rivals and make money at it.

Subaru's successful brand strategy and ad campaign featuring Australian Paul Hogan who portrayed Crocodile Dundee in the movie of the same name, was combined with the Australian name ("sub-brand") "Outback" to create the integration between the strategy, the product and the brand. Subaru is now a profitable and well-respected niche competitor, a growing brand with a clearly defined brand image and character.

A popular graphical way to portray brand strategy is with the four-square matrix:

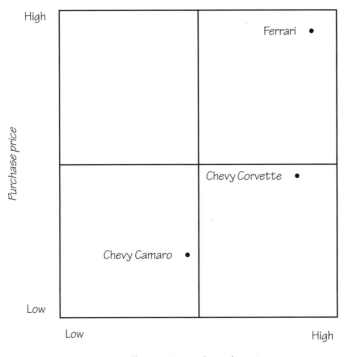

High

Purchase price

Ferrari •

Chevy Corvette •

Chevy Camaro •

Low

Low   High

Engine size and acceleration

You can use a matrix like this to convey useful information about relative features and brand issues in a single graphic tool. These matrices are frequently used by consultants and academics. This type of matrix was overused at times in the 1980s, but superb consulting organizations like the Boston Consulting Group used such tools as the centerpiece of portfolio management and strategy portrayal very successfully. Here's how you can use a matrix like this to show brand attributes and the ranges of competing product or services in a simple, visual and comparative fashion. In the example above, three well known cars are plotted. The very expensive

Ferrari, which can accelerate from 0–60 mph in about 5 seconds, the Chevrolet Corvette which costs only a fraction of the Ferrari's price, but is almost as fast, and the much less expensive Chevrolet Camaro, which can also be equipped for fast acceleration.

> **Smart things to say about brands**
>
> For the best results, the brand strategy and the company strategy must match closely.

You could choose many other brand features such as luxury amenities, gas mileage, warranties, and so forth to portray this way. This device is especially useful because your brand strategies do not exist in a vacuum. Consumers are always comparing alternative purchases, and using brands to help them find the value proposition upon which their decision will be based. I used similar graphical analyses, including the Shape of Value™ approach explained in my earlier book *The Shape Shifters* (Wiley 1997) to help brand managers spot gaps in markets that their new brands could fill, and see weaknesses that better be strengthened.

Companies create brands, for a variety of reasons – sometimes on purpose and occasionally accidentally. Ben & Jerry's ice-cream brand came from the hippie-like founders' names, and the company was environmentally conscious and egalitarian like its founders. WD-40, the highly successful household lubricant, was named after a combination of its intended purpose when first developed: WD = Water Displacement (i.e. to protect electronic components from damage by water) and the fact that the successful formula was the 40th one tested!

> **Smart things to say about brands**

Egotists who think they are smarter than the customer will lose every time – especially to humble people who know they aren't. Go, talk to customers, ask them what they think and then listen to what they have to say.

> A clear and effective brand identity, one for which there is understanding and buy-in throughout the organization, should be linked to the business's vision and its organizational culture and values. It should provide guidance as to which programs and communications will support and reinforce the brand and which will detract and confuse.
>
> Erich Joachimsthaler and David Aaker, "Building Brands Without Mass Media" in *Harvard Business Review*, January–February 1997

Smart quotes

Brands such as Ben & Jerry's, when successful, have distinctive brand characters and brand images associated with them. Many brands are simply the names of the founders who, after accumulating the goodwill of their customers for years, come to be symbolic of a specific type of value, and a pattern of reliable behavior. A couple of the most familiar brand examples of this type are Ford and Chrysler, both leading US auto companies named after their founders. These founders, their successors and their companies assume the brand character and image that their products and conduct earned them over the years. If your brand is either a "no-name brand" (like the EG&G example) or a brand that is tainted by some highly publicized failures (like the Yugo auto, which was known for its poor quality and unreliable performance) then you may need to start with a clean slate.

A strategy is too important to delegate

Many companies delegate strategy to brand managers. This is wrong. Brand managers can refine and improve strategy. They can assure that it is consistently followed. They are not the right ones to initiate and institutionalize it. The development of a strategy for a brand that is the symbol of an important part of a company belongs in the hands of someone who has the clout and influence (and incentives) to think strategically on a larger scale than just one brand.

Every major action you take in a business should have a strategic reason or purpose behind it. This is especially true when it comes to brand-name creation, selection and promotion. Brands seldom just materialize out of thin air. Picking them is not easy. Developing them is time-consuming and expensive. Don't take these jobs lightly.

The first step in developing a Brand Strategy is to find out what, exactly it is that your current brand (assuming you have one) means to consumers and intermediate (trade) customers, and how well known it is. Such a step usually involves a survey, done with statistical accuracy against the audience or population you care about. This is a job for professionals. Doing the market research survey poorly or wrong can lead to major investments of time and money on flawed premises – which usually leads to disastrous results.

One of the most important jobs of a smart brand manager is to carefully consider the strategy underlying the brand before plunging headlong into trying to create, build and establish a brand. More brands fail because this step was omitted or too little attention was given to it.

Most advertising agencies either do this kind of brand awareness and image survey or have associated market research firms who specialize in doing such surveys. I will discuss brand awareness further in a later chapter, but the essence of this term is how many people recognize your brand name, with and without prompting. Then how many of those have any idea what the brand name stands for. Once you know this information, you know the size of the task ahead of you.

The next step you must take is to determine what are the strategies of your company (overall) and what its marketing efforts should consist of – especially with regard to brands and branding. It is amazing how many companies skip right past this step and go to the advertising part of the tactical plans, because that part is more fun! Unfortunately unless you give proper attention to corporate strategy and a well-defined, tightly integrated marketing plan, the advertising money you spend may be wasted, and certainly will have less than the desired effect.

The third step you must take is to decide what you want your brand to mean and convey – and whether that can be achieved given the findings and decisions of the two preceding steps. The importance of being realistic about expectations is something you cannot overlook when developing brands. Once these criteria have been met, there are critical details to pursue:

- developing a brand strategy

- creating a desired brand image

- establishing the specific brand character or personality chosen.

New brand successes

A part of a brand strategy is understanding and/or developing a brand character for your brand. Do you want your brand to be robust or subtle, strong or gentle, fast or relaxed, etc.? There are probably many theoretical options here, but fewer that are actually viable if your brand is not a totally new one. If it is a new one, the choices are wide open.

All brands that have been in existence for some time, have developed some kind of "character" already – the only question is whether that will be the right one for your marketing plans. When a new brand is being developed, the character and the brand name can be developed together – a desirable, but usually more expensive and time-consuming proposition.

Lexus and Acura autos were new brands, created and developed to serve a luxury market in the US. Acura was chosen at least partly because Honda wanted to convey the image of precision and accuracy in the vehicle at a time when competing US and German luxury cars were visiting the repair shop too often. Honda's engineering of the Acura matched the "precision" brand character in the tight, accurate driving feeling and the precise fit of the parts of the car. The model names even cried out legendary precision: the "Legend" and the "Integra" (as in integral – another precision-like term).

Lexus was right on the heels of Acura, as Toyota aimed for (and hit) the heart of the luxury market with their initial offerings. Lexus and the target market were similar words, thus conveying the product's promise – a luxurious auto. The products delivered on the promise of their names. Separate dealerships were established to support the promise of the brand precision and/or luxury brand names. These Japanese entrants rapidly took volume from Cadillac, Lincoln, Mercedes and BMW in the US market. Everything from promotional literature to TV ads emphasized equal luxury and better quality than US competitors, and at prices far below German competition.

Only when Acura abandoned the well known and highly regarded Legend (sub-brand) and made some product mediocrity errors were the German luxury makers, BMW and Mercedes able to regain lost sales and scramble back to the earlier prestige leadership positions.

Smart things to say about brands

Don't get lost in "semantics". Decide what you want your brand stand for, to mean and what mental picture you want to place in the mind of purchasers – and make sure you stay on that course.

Brand image or brand identity

There are a lot of terms used to describe the various aspects of brands that are important. I will try to group the terms somewhat to ease understanding, as long as you realize that purists will crucify me for polluting their pure definitions. The real world is not a very pure or theoretical place, and what is important is that there is a common understanding about why brands are important, and what the various aspects of them mean to the owner, the advertiser, and above all, to the consumer.

These two terms – *brand image* and *brand identity* are similar, in that they both describe many facets of the brand. The brand image or identity can be described as an aspect of a product, and/or an organization, and/or a personality, and/or a symbol with the associated visual imagery and icons. The semantics of which term to use should not get in the way of understanding what is important about a brand – what it means to the potential purchasers! Because of this confusing semantic soup, most of the valuable messages in this book will be illustrated with stories of real world situations and outcomes. After a brief attempt to separate and define its ingredients, the semantic soup will be stirred well, and then left to congeal.

Smart quotes

It depends on which book or which professor you ask, which set of terms you get.

Gary Medalis (Advertising V.P. Manco, Inc.)

- Can you define brand character, brand image, brand identity, brand position, brand personality, and brand equity?
- What is the likelihood of getting two people, especially brand "experts," to come up with similar definitions?
- How can you cope with listening to too many experts and not getting confused with semantics and terms?

KILLER QUESTIONS

Identity building of brands

A simple example of how a brand can be built by association and careful attention to its identity might be in order here. Simple recognition is very powerful. People often like well-known brands just because they are well known! When that knowledge is associated with the right kind of identity, the well-known brand becomes one with a specific identity. What do you think of when you hear about Hugo Boss clothing? If you are the typical consumer, you think of a prestigious clothing brand. You may have never bought or even shopped for Hugo Boss clothes – their distribution is decidedly limited on purpose – to elite retail outlets.

Hugo Boss built much of this image without major advertising media expenditures. But, they sponsored Porsche's Formula One racing efforts and thus tagged along with Porsche's strong exclusive international image. International tennis and ski sponsorships also elevated Hugo Boss' image by being present only in venues consistent with the identity desired. In a 1991 survey of men's clothing brands by the German magazine *Gehobener Lebensstil*, Hugo Boss was the highest ranked brand for having an aura of exclusivity.

KILLER QUESTIONS

What is the desired image of identity for our brand?

Polo Ralph Lauren created an entirely new and paradoxical market in high-fashion clothing by basing it on the lack of fashion! What? Right! Polo clothing is distinctively like what you used to wear to go to the store, work in the yard or wash the car, but with the aura of a haute couture designer's name and logo. Lauren took cues from classic lines like Burberry's, Aquascutum and Brook Brothers, but took them to a new level of casual chic. These classic styles mean less product obsolescence, which means the price premium can be a little less and the profit premium a little more than comparable high fashion lines.

Lauren has built and owns a niche between haute couture and older classic lines by using its designer name, elegant stores, luxury materials and a timeless classic look. This captured share from neighboring brands and created new customers who were put off by the price levels of the other high-end lines and the lack of brand cachet of lower niche competitors. With annual sales that exceed $5 billion worldwide, Polo Ralph Lauren is the first American fashion design house to take its clothing sales global on such a large scale, yet remain decidedly upscale in its niche. How can you tell? Go to the Pacific Rim countries (Taiwan, Korea, Hong Kong, etc.) and see which brands they are selling on the streets as counterfeits and knockoffs – Polo is one of them!

Choosing a brand name

Entire books could be written about this, and fortunes made or lost in the actual choice of a brand name. Ford's now infamous Edsel automobile was named after one of the Ford family. Was it a bad name? Not necessarily, but it wasn't a good one either. What is an Edsel? It communicates nothing about what to expect of the product, why it is different, better,

Q: Why not just choose any name and push it until it is accepted as a brand for a product or service?

A: Because the human mind forms mental pictures when it hears certain words and, if the picture and the words associated with the brand name don't match or are in conflict, the consumer's mind will reject the image. *Example:* Lexus was not a good brand name for an economy-car line – the name is (intentionally) too similar to the familiar word "luxury." But it was an excellent choice for a luxury product.

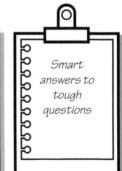

Smart answers to tough questions

more fun or anything at all. It is just a name. Like no-name companies that simply use their initials, the entire image and identity of the brand must be

Smart things
to say about
brands

- *A company brand name should suggest stability and integrity.*
  Wouldn't you rather buy insurance or securities from a company named Prudential than one named CIGNA? What's a CIGNA? At least Prudential might be prudent about investing your money.
- *A product brand name should communicate something about the product.*
  Weathershield is a better name for a window than Pella, even though Pella makes superb windows. Soft-Touch is a better name for a car wash than Calibur, even though both use the same process.
- *A name should avoid negative imagery or identification.*
  AYDs weight-loss candy was doomed as soon as the Acquired Immune Deficiency Syndrome became widespread and was known as AIDs! Chevrolet's "Nova" means "don't go" in some languages – which is a bad name for a car.
- *Avoid acronyms whenever possible.*
  You can buy a PC from IBM, and know what it means, but many companies and acronyms are meaningless to most consumers. What is an EG&G?
- *Naming products after people has been successful in the past.*
  Betty Crocker, Duncan Hines, Charles Schwab, Ralph Lauren and many others convey brand images in keeping with the products and companies that carry their names.
- *Fun, upbeat, active and cheerful names do better than bland or (ugh) corporate-sounding names.*
  Cheerios and Life are friendlier-sounding than All-Bran or Mueslix. A Mustang or Thunderbird would certainly be more exciting to ride in than a Contour or a Catera. (What the heck is a Catera?)
- *Don't use generic names, or allow the brand name to become part of the vernacular – it will not be protectable.*
  Nylon and Aspirin became so common the companies who originated them lost their trademark protection. The Computer Store is too generic to be protected, as are names like "Fresh Bread."

built from scratch. This is a daunting task, and an expensive one. On the other hand consider Acura and Lexus. One might infer that Acuras were accurate about something and the Lexuses were luxurious. This is exactly what Honda and Toyota, the Japanese companies that created these brands, intended.

Developing brands and segmentation

Another brand name, which became prominent, was the result of a targeted strategic marketing effort on behalf of a previously undifferentiated product – vodka. Absolut vodka was a Swedish product that was imported into the US in an era when that was not the perceived source for notable vodka brands (*Russia* was: with Smirnoff, Stolichnaya, etc.) Absolut knew that differentiating their vodka based on ingredients was a losing battle.

They chose to differentiate it on Brand Image & Personality. Its bottle was unusual and distinctively shaped compared with competing brands, and they chose this shape as an icon around which they built an entire brand-image campaign supported by innovative print advertising. Even the simple, plain all-upper-case graphics supported the minimalist appeal that created a focus of attention on the shape of the clear bottle.

Successful segmentation of a brand

Building a strategy around a brand image or identity may seem backward, but in this case it was highly effective. A similar brand image/identity strategy was used by GAP, but its was more carefully integrated to an overall corporate strategy. GAP has already succeeded with its store look and feel when it acquired the Banana Republic chain in 1983. GAP had successfully married a rapid-distribution strategy with simple, timeless clothing designs to become a destination store and brand for many shoppers.

GAP's value has little to do with the historical cost of its store fixtures and everything to do with something accounting ignores: its brand image, based on a feel for the market and carefully nurtured with advertising.

Bernard Condon, *Forbes* magazine, January 1999

As GAP grew more fashion forward, and as Banana Republic's "safari-style" of clothing moved increasingly out of the popular mainstream, the need for segmentation of products and brands became evident. So also did the need for a lower-cost, more-popularly priced line of clothing, to be sold outside GAP's and Banana Republic's pricey, high-rent mall locations. Thus GAP created Old Navy. Major wars had been over for several decades, thus the "army/navy surplus" stores that flourished in the 1950s and 1960s had all but disappeared. All that was left was their memory of affordable, durable, but not-too-stylish clothing – a perfect downscale image for GAP. A natural (good) extension of the GAP brand name was also Baby GAP. (Many brand extensions are bad ideas – more on that later.)

The result: four brands, each carving out a specific image segment for itself: Banana Republic was repositioned to be the high end, Old Navy spread through strip malls and took the low-end, value image, Baby GAP had clothes for the small children of loyal GAP shoppers, and GAP anchored itself solidly in the fashion forward middle, rotating its lines several times a year capitalizing on its distribution system's capability to handle such frequent merchandise shifts. The corporate strategy was clearly driving the brand strategy; all built around the segmented brand images.

Brand image misadventures and mistakes

The subtitle of this could be "the bigger they are, the dumber things they do, and then do again." A backfired brand strategy was that of the Cadillac division of GM. More than a decade ago, someone had the idea that Cadillac needed a small car. That was the first mistake. If only they had done their homework. (That's called consumer market research – something only discovered in recent history at GM – before that they believed they "made the market" so they didn't do much consumer research.) GM might have discovered that people's picture of the Cadillac motor car was a big, roomy, soft riding, quiet, feature laden, luxury car – and a status symbol.

What did Cadillac do? They took a lowly Chevrolet Cavalier – not a particularly good car to start with – and dressed it up in Cadillac trim. Chrome, luxury options, leather, and of course the Cadillac emblem on the grille were their idea of making a small, cramped, poor riding, noisy, but feature laden, wanna-be luxury car a Cadillac. Of course the public wasn't fooled. You could buy a Cadillac emblem at the repair shop and stick it on any car you wanted, but that didn't make it a Cadillac. It did make the folks at Cadillac look pretty silly, though.

> *Smart things to say about brands*
>
> Don't forget or become misled about what your brand stands for – and what it doesn't stand for – with consumers.

Then, just when GM were showing signs of improving their marketing and brand management, they took the Opel – a fine European mid-size sedan – and did it again. The Opel was at least a worthy try, because it was a good vehicle. But Catera looked way too much like its US sister cars from the GM design studios – the Saturn (at less than half the price) and the similarly sized, not too exciting Chevrolet Lumina – a pedestrian vehicle also selling at nearly half the Catera's price, that could easily get confused in a parking lot with your new Cadillac Catera! Then the ad campaign – "the Caddy that zigs" – with a weird little duck as the mascot was as far off the mark as the car. Who were they kidding? This was no Cadillac – and everybody (but Cadillac) knew it!

The Catera had some of the hottest lease deals on the market and barely made a scratch or a dent in the sales of the velvety smooth Lexus ES300 or the nimble and quick BMW 3 series. Brand image and identity plus the brand's character and personality all work together to define what a product is and what it isn't. When you try to turn a sow's ear into a silk purse, even a legendary brand like Cadillac can't fool consumers.

If only Cadillac had kept refining the original Seville STS with the Northstar power train system. That was a unique and consistent display of Cadillac's brand image and personality. A contemporarily styled, large, roomy, luxurious, powerful, prestigious, and good road-handling car was exactly the right brand image for a "new" Cadillac. Only now, three years later, are they moving back in that direction. Not too surprisingly, their late-to-market large sport utility vehicle, Escalade is an early success. Why? Think about the brand's image. It is a large, spacious, luxurious, status-symbol vehicle. Surprise – No!

Brand character, position and personality

Brand positioning

One of the most popular and influential books of the 1980s was *Positioning – The Battle for your Mind* by Al Ries and Jack Trout. I don't intend to duplicate its content here, but a few comments on positioning a brand are required.

> Positioning starts with a product. A piece of merchandise, a service, a company, an institution, or even a person ... But positioning is not what you do with the product. Positioning is what you do to the mind of the prospect. That is, you position the product in the mind of the prospect.
>
> Al Ries and Jack Trout

Smart quotes

How's that for an opinion on the importance of brand name? Pretty strong words, but right on the mark. Was Shakespeare wrong? Would a rose by any other name smell as sweet? Maybe not! This positioning concept has definite merit in building a brand. The name must fit the positioning and vice-versa. If it doesn't, a change is required – and fast!

There are many ways to describe brand positioning. I have chosen just one set of factors to illustrate the concept of positioning. There is nothing magic about this set other than it covers the most common themes. Ries & Trout's book *Positioning* and subsequent ones by those two authors cover this topic very extensively – although not always objectively – they are opinionated about what works and what doesn't.

Smart quotes

> Positioning is at the very center of creating and building brand equity ... If brand equity is the perceived value of the product – how people think of the product or service on its own and relative to competition – then that perceived value basically describes the 'position' in their minds.
>
> Joe Marconi, *Beyond Branding* (Probus Publishing, Chicago, IL, 1993)

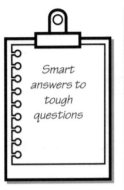

Q: What are the most prominent types of positioning for brands?

A: There are lots of them, but here are a few of the best ones to know.

- *Value positioning:* This is used by brands that are not in the lowest price ranges, but would like to convince consumers that they have a high ratio of features to price.

- *Comparative Positioning:* This exists where one brand attempts to convince a consumer that it is a better choice than another brand or set of comparable brands.

- *Unique Attribute Positioning:* A brand uses a specific or unique attribute to distinguish itself and/or to get the consumer to choose it over other alternative brands that may or may not have this attribute.

- *Meaningless Attribute Positioning:* In this case a brand claims superiority on an attribute which is meaningless, or relatively unimportant from an objective standpoint. This actually works well in real-life applications.

- *Fame or Celebrity Positioning:* In this case the brand is positioned as connected to an event, a person, or something or someone famous, such as a celebrity endorser, or a major sporting event, etc.

Beware of authors (including myself) who take positions unsupported by facts. Gather your own data, form your own opinions and use your own brain.

Building a new completely brand

The subtitle of this one could be, if you do something right, mess with it until you foul it up! That is exactly what GM is in danger of doing to Saturn. While GM was botching up the Cadillac brand with its misguided new vehicles, it was doing one brand right – albeit not very profitably. Saturn was GM's launch of a new car, a new brand, and whole new company to compete with Japanese imports. The brand building part of this was a huge success. So was the team-based production plant and product quality resulting. Unfortunately, the Saturn project has never been consistently profitable.

Launched amidst much fanfare in 1985, Saturn was a noble experiment in GM's corporate mish-mash of car lines. The brand theme: "A Different Kind of Company, A Different Kind of Car" was perfect. The brand's supporting elements – dealerships that were actually friendly, no-hassle pricing, personalization of the purchase (complete with pictures of the people who made the cars and bought the cars) – all led to a huge consumer success. In a few short years, Saturn climbed to the top ranks of customer satisfaction and brand recognition surveys.

Saturn was masterful in creating associations with the brand. People felt that this was a car built for them, by people who cared, sold by dealers who cared, and serviced by technicians who cared about the customers – them! Saturn even staged "homecoming" picnics at their Spring Hill, TN plant for Saturn buyers, who came from far and wide to be a part of this uniquely "different kind of company." Strong brands usually go beyond the product's physical attributes to create a brand image, personality and relationship with customers that make them loyal supporters.

The only problem thus far is that parent GM viewed this as an experiment and the success in the brand and market position was not paralleled in the financial success. The rebellious child of GM, that proved so popular with consumers, didn't make enough money for the huge investment. The strategy was not well enough thought out up-front to expand the brand franchise and capitalize on the potential of the success.

Another new brand does it right – from the start

This one could have a subtitle too. If you have enough money and spend it wisely, you end up with a good result! For a model discussion of Brand Character, Position and Personality, the newly created powerhouse in network communications, Lucent Technologies is an excellent example. Lucent had only a few months to develop a new brand name for what was once was the manufacturing arm of AT&T and the prestigious Bell Labs. With its long history of innovation, there was a distinctive brand character, a clutter-breaking identity, which was essential in the position and personality of the new brand name.

Landor & Associates were retained to come up with the new name and the visual identity that accompanied it. The strategy was to carefully avoid the name branding them as "just another telephone company" like the Baby Bells and many others. In addition, they wanted to avoid the often used blue, gray and black colors commonly identified with other leading electronics companies like IBM, Microsoft, Sony, Texas Instruments, GE, and Motorola.

Names containing telephonic, high-tech components like "sys," "tech," "net," and of course "tel," were also avoided. Lucent wanted to shed part of the AT&T image, that of slowness and inflexible arrogance. It also wanted to add new images of speed, energy, focus and vision to the good parts of its old association with AT&T – reliability, technology, and experience.

Thus "Lucent" – which means "glowing with light" and "marked by clarity" was chosen to go with the modifier "Technologies" (which can be dropped later) and was incorporated with the subtitle "Bell Labs Innovations" to retain the innovative tie-in to the old parent.

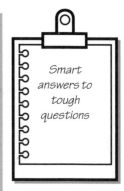
A new icon – a red-on-white (or white-on-red) – ring symbolized innovation, motion and completeness, and the hand-drawn aspect of the ring symbolized "the creativity of the people". A massive introductory advertising campaign allowed Lucent to reach 91% awareness in six months in the financial community – one of its key constituencies because it needed to retain investor confidence until its new identity was more widespread with consumers and the general public (as it is now).

That Lucent's brand character and position goals were achieved is evident by the widespread acceptance and memorable association with the desired brand meanings. For every success story like this, there are, unfortunately multiple failures. Yet, the task must be done; the challenge must be taken up. Brands are the beacons that show the way for customers to find the particular value they desire and identify who can provide that value.

What works for one brand, may not work for another

Smart things
to say about brands

Make sure you understand why something works in one brand situation, and how another brand situation is different. "Different strokes for different folks" applies to brand strategy too.

If it seems that I am picking on General Motors, maybe I am. GM is very large and have done more than their share of dumb things with their brands over the past few decades. Here they go again! It seems they continue to do dumb things!

Positioning a brand relative to other brands is risky at best and foolish are worst. Car-rental company Avis made it work with their "We're number 1 – we try harder" campaign. It had an honest ring to it and made a promise that was believable. The public went for it and Avis grew – but they didn't make number 1. That is the problem with brand campaigns like theirs, but they still did pretty well. GM, on the other hand, did it the dumb way.

GM's Buick division was rightfully proud to make the top ten list of cars in J.D. Power's annual quality ranking. This was at a time when the list was dominated by Japanese and a few German luxury car brands. Buick came in number 5! Good for them!

What did GM do? They made a big deal of it. What did consumers do? They yawned, and thought, "number 5 – that's not so hot!" Then they went out and bought cars from Honda/Acura, Toyota/Lexus, and Nissan/Infiniti in record quantities. Do you want to guess who was number 1, 2, 3, and 4 on the list? Never mind – you know the answer!

As if this example isn't bad enough, GM may be the poster-child for meaningless brand proliferation. At least that is what its leading competitors

DaimlerChrysler and BMW think. How can Buick reasonably expect to compete while supporting so many sub-brands: Century, Regal, LeSabre, and Park Avenue? Alfred Sloan built GM on the theory of car divisions each focused on a clear class of consumer. Over the years, GM has polluted his original idea by having most of the divisions making overlapping

The power of brand equity

There are many numbers in an annual report which attempt to describe a company's assets and shareholder equity. But one of the numbers you don't find is a number that may be a company's biggest asset – its brand equity.

Although not always apparent, the most important assets of a firm are intangible. These assets may include brands, symbols, slogans, training manuals, processes, people skills and other items which define the company and its positions in the minds of consumers. Few, if any of these show up on a firm's balance sheet, but when the asset value of these items exceeds the cost of developing them, a firm has valuable brand equity. Brand equity involves brand loyalty, brand awareness, perceived quality, brand associations, and other brand assets.

Brand equity gives value to customers. This value is achieved by helping customers process information about the marketplace and gain confidence in their purchase decisions. Ultimately brand equity enhances consumer satisfaction when using the product.

Brand equity gives value to the firm by increasing the effectiveness of marketing programs. The components of brand equity allow a firm to develop a competitive advantage over other firms. Ultimately that leads to higher price earnings ratios and enhanced shareholder value, achieved because of the brand loyalty of customers.

Dr Roger D. Blackwell

vehicles under their primary brand and a proliferation of sub-brands. Who can keep them all straight, let alone decide that they want one of them?

KILLER QUESTIONS

Will this brand image/
identity, character,
and personality
yield valuable brand
equity if we create
it successfully?

As if Buick's proliferation is not enough, add Oldsmobile's Alero, Intrigue, and Aurora (do they even still sell the old Delta 88?). All of these products blanket essentially the same consumers in specifications, price, target ages, demographics and more. While Oldsmobile has tried to depart from its stodgy image, one suspects that an ad theme: "this is not your father's Oldsmobile" really means, "this is pretty much your father's Oldsmobile, but we just want you to buy it while you are in your 30s anyway." Who are they kidding? Give me a BMW, a Volvo, a Saab, or even a Japanese mid-priced quasi-luxury sedan – Toyota Camry or Honda Accord, loaded with options, or a base Lexus or Acura – any day! Ironically, only after the old "not your father's Oldsmobile" campaign died, did Oldsmobile actually come up with a group of fresh new cars, the Alero, Intrigue, and Aurora. A smart brand manager never forgets, timing is everything!

Brand Equity

Brand equity is the umbrella of outcomes

I know many brilliant professors, but, if you take them all too seriously and listen too closely, they will confuse you beyond belief. I will try to not let that happen here, because there are some smart things to know that a special few of these professors can help us with. Try not to get tangled up in the jargon, but think about what it all means: "buy mine, not the other guy's!"

Defining brand equity

Brand Equity is a set of assets (and liabilities) linked to a brand's name and symbol that adds to (or subtracts from) the value provided by a product or service to a firm and/or that firm's customers. The major brand asset categories are:
- brand-name awareness
- brand loyalty
- perceived quality
- brand associations

Professor David A. Aaker

Many experts use the term *Brand Equity*, but few know exactly what it means. Dr Roger Blackwell is one of the few. He describes the power of brand equity and in doing so, mentions several of its key components. Professor David Aaker, who has written extensively on Brand Equity, offers a simple, useful definition.

Brand character, position, personality, image and identity are semantically confusing enough, but now brand equity too? Well, brand equity is an important term for the smart brand-builder to understand thoroughly because it provides a valuation umbrella for the outcomes of all the other brand semantics terms.

Q: What kind of awareness, loyalty, perceptions and associations result from creating a brand with a given image, identity, character, position and personality?

A: The name given for the outcome – the total of the value of the awareness, loyalty, perceptions and associations – is brand equity.

Smart things
to say about
brands

Marketing managers must understand the importance and value of their brand's equity when they ask for (or justify) resources (money mostly) to support that brand. Nothing dies faster than a brand that is not supported properly. Consumers have short memories and are flooded with new brands on which to spend their money.

Maybe a simpler way to say it is: after you have built the brand name, brand equity is what you actually own. Just like the raw piece of property that you buy, clear, grade, and then build a house upon, equity is the outcome. You bought dirt, labor, building materials and so forth, but your equity is in the finished building – a home – that resulted.

Brand equity is the combination of brand awareness and loyalty, consumer perceptions and associations that are taken away in the minds of purchasers of the brand. Just as mortgage payments on the house continue to build equity, so also do brand development and support investments.

Smart quotes

The old saying was right, "The truth will set you free" – but what it didn't say was "you will suffer while it does."

Michael Bozic (former President of Sears and Hills, now Sr. Vice President of Kmart)

What Lucent is building can be valued as brand equity, but the more obvious and measurable aspects of brand awareness, brand preference and brand loyalty, are more meaningful to most people. Because of this, I will try to be careful with these terms and describe most of the Smart Things to Know in terms of examples that illustrate the points and eliminate "semantic-soup" misunderstandings.

Brand equity valuation is important

We all know there is a relationship between advertising investment and the brand value or brand equity that results. The question is, "what is that

Smart quotes

It is simply not good enough to propose that the high cost (of advertising) will be worth the investment. Decision makers need more convincing evidence.

Raj Aggarwal (Edward J. and Louis E. Mellen Chair of Finance, John Carroll University, Cleveland), Irene M. Herremans (University of Calgary), John K. Ryans (Bridgestone Professor of International Business, Kent State University), "Toward Improved Marketing Performance Measures: a Study of the Relationship Between Advertising and Brand Value"

relationship?" Intuitively, we can assume that there is a wide variation in how effectively and efficiently advertisers use their resources to build brand equity.

As I was writing this section, I raised this topic with Professor Raj Aggarwal. Raj shared with me some recent research work undertaken with colleagues. While the paper includes much more numerical detail than is suitable for this book, a few of its conclusions are valuable. As part of their work, they identified a series of brand equity measures, most of which I have covered already or are shown in the insets. The conclusions most useful to smart individuals are given below.

Their analysis concentrated on three key factors that tend to drive brand value and the resulting cash flows: marketing investment, quality of product, and market share. By carefully analyzing these factors and related expenditures in advertising against published brand equity values over a longer time frame (5–10 years) they concluded that just spending money is not the answer. There is a wide variation in how effectively expenditures translate into brand equity, and although in its infancy, the means to measure the results are now emerging.

To eliminate the pressure for short-term results especially when budgets are tight, it is essential that managers can show that a cut in advertising expenditures will be detrimental to the bottom-line profitability in the longer run.

Raj Aggarwal (Edward J. and Louis E. Mellen Chair of Finance, John Carroll University, Cleveland), Irene M. Herremans (University of Calgary), John K. Ryans (Bridgestone Professor of International Business, Kent State University)

Before we go on, let's summarize. First define the strategy – both corporate and marketing – then the strategy for the brand. Don't make the Saturn mistake and have a brand success and an economic failure. Find out what the brand's perception is now (if there is an existing brand), and define what you want it to be, or how you want the new brand to differ.

Then be realistic if you can get from here to there in the time frame available and with the resources you are willing to commit. If the answer is still to push ahead, then tackle the brand image and character issues and get going – the competition is not standing still!

Since the initial premise of our topic of brands and branding is that brands are valuable and advantageous, let's get on with how and why – the benefits of a brand.

3

A Brand's Benefits

WHY GO TO THE TROUBLE TO CREATE AND USE A BRAND NAME – WHO CARES?

Consumers care, and they vote with money for the brand they care most about. Brands help companies identify products and services in unique ways that differentiate them from competitors in the minds of consumers. Globalization increases a strong brand's importance when it bridges language and culture barriers.

Brand benefits

Now that we have thoroughly trashed the people who thought they could just pick a name at random and build on it, let's kick around the benefits of doing it right. There must be some good reasons to go to the trouble of branding products and services, and there are!

1. You make a lot of money.

2. You make even more money.

3. You keep on making money! But:

4. It takes money to make money.

Smart quotes

There's a
sucker born
every minute.

P.T. Barnum

That's why spending the start-up money wisely is a smart thing to do. Advertising and promotion to build a brand is a long-term investment, not a short-term expense – don't let myopic money managers tell you different just because of arcane accounting rules.

In this chapter, we will cover why it is smart to build a brand. You'll want to pay close attention, because these will be many of the answers you need to give the budget cutters when they sharpen the pencils to go after the advertising and promotions budget in the misguided hope to temporarily improve the bottom line. A common mistake is to make the current quarter and the next one at the expense of the next 8–12 quarters. Strong brands increase sales and profits, and good advertising builds strong brands.

Smart quotes

Companies with recognized
brands like amazon.com and
the GAP are well known and
are viewed as trusted ven-
dors.

Derek Brown (Internet
analyst for Volpe, Brown,
Whelan & Co.)

Done right, some of the brand benefits are price premiums, higher profits, repeat purchases and a sales advantage over competitors in close decisions. And these are just a few of the benefits. A company's value with investors and security analysts is another benefit of a highly recognized and preferred brand name. The money managers may understand that one!

Why create and build brands?

They say "fools rush in where angels fear to tread." A lot of fools create brands without first thinking for more than a few hours (often less) about what they hope to do with them. This section is for them – and for all of the serious-minded readers who may have wondered in an idle moment about why do we need to build a brand at all? Much of this rational has been scattered about or mentioned in the prior chapters, and will be covered in more detail in chapters to come. I am putting it here in one place for lazy browsers and serious strategists – they are often not far apart in their motivations – good results with economy of effort and time!

Brands identify and differentiate. The more they do this, the more valuable they are in targeting consumers and purchasers. Brands provide an implied guarantee of sorts to consumers – of the quality, service, value and innovation contained in the goods and services they represent.

Let's do a quick test: Gucci. What picture comes to mind? (*Exclusive, stylish, expensive accessories?*) See, it works!

Brands also provide the basis for relationships between the brand owner and the purchaser. This is especially important for service providers. Internet brands seek to establish these relationships to ensure repeat visits to their web sites – this is the e-commerce parallel of brand loyalty.

Another quick test: Yahoo! What picture comes to mind? (*A web-site portal that offers one-stop access to a wide variety of products, services and information on the Internet?*) Good, you got it right!

A brand is a paradox

A brand can easily confuse the uninformed brand builder because there are aspects of brands that are both blessings and curses. Brands can be incredibly strong and amazingly fragile. Ed Holzer, Chairman of Lois EJL advertising relates some examples of how a brand can be used and abused.

Cadillac (GM again!) misapplied its brand name on the Allante' sport coupe in hopes of appealing to a younger, affluent group of consumers. This not only failed with Allante', but irritated and turned off traditional Cadillac customers who were a generation older – a lose-lose proposition. This not only did not capitalize on the Cadillac brand name because the brand didn't translate well to this use, but ultimately hurt the Cadillac brand by the misapplication to a product that didn't fit the brand's image. Such a move not only confuses the brand's image, but wastes resources and dilutes the brand message.

Another example of misapplication of a brand to no benefit is described by Holzer as "carrying a good thing too far." First Alert was the market leader in smoke detectors with over 80% share of market at the time. When the brand was extended to fire extinguishers and carbon monoxide detectors, consumers understood the application of the brand name because it made sense to them. Then First Alert tried to extend the brand to children's safety products and failed with it. There was not enough meaningful transfer of the brand's identity to this category, thus resources were wasted because the brand was misapplied.

Smart quotes

A strong brand can be your best friend and your worst enemy. It is your best friend because it is one of the most powerful tools you can use to get consumer sales. It becomes your worst enemy when you do one of two things to it: you misapply it, or you forget how fragile it is and you damage it.

Ed Holzer (Chairman, Lois EJL Advertising)

Brand value

An investor's perspective on why branding matters

The well-known investment firm, PaineWebber (PW) produces a lot of informative research material for its investors. A recent publication entitled *Hardlines Retailing – Why Branding Matters* provides a useful thought model on branding and a number of insights about why this whole issue of branding is very important. Although it is focused on retail, hardlines products and the US market, the thought processes are applicable to other markets and products/services.

For those who have forgotten, business is a game where the score is kept in money. The prize is to do well enough to play again – over and over – making even more money. While PaineWebber's study is focused on the US retail marketplace, globalization of many retailing trends is proceeding so rapidly that lessons from the US will be useful in many other world markets. As this is being written, Wal*Mart is aggressively expanding in Europe via acquisitions. The branded product landscape in Europe will change substantially as a result of this retail invasion.

> Smart things
> to say about brands
>
> Business is a game where the
> score is kept in money!

The first point of interest in the PW study is that retail consolidation cycles continue to compress. This is true in all markets, not just the US, but American retailing provides good lessons for other parts of the world to learn from and build upon.

In the US, department stores took over 100 years for consolidation to take hold, and reduce the number of major participants to just a handful. Supermarkets took 80 years, and are far from complete as "supercenters" blur the boundaries of the industry and take share in huge gulps. Discount stores took only 30 years for the industry to shake out smaller regional chains until 75% of these retail sales are in the hands of the big three: Wal*Mart, Kmart, and Target.

These models vary from country to country in Europe: some are further down the retailing evolutionary curve than others (France), and some simply will always lag others (Italy). US Warehouse clubs in the US took only 20 years to consolidate to Costco, Sam's and BJ's. Home improvement super-centers took only 15 years, to get down to half a dozen, led by Home Depot and Lowe's. Office Products Superstores took just 10 years for Office Depot, Staples and OfficeMax to emerge as the survivors.

> **Smart things to say about brands**
>
> The difference-making brands may be those of highly desirable products – or they may be those of highly desirable and successful stores.

Internet retailing will add yet its own definition of speed. The Internet has only existed as a consumer/brand phenomenon for five years – since the advent of Netscape's (Mosaic-based) browser starting in 1995. Many new retail concepts are still unproven. Carmax, AutoNation, amazon.com, KidsRUs, Home Depot's EXPO, and even such "old" chains as Sports Authority (now just over 10 years old) have yet to prove their long term financial viability.

The punch line you have been waiting for is buried in all of this retail information is that brands are what will make the ultimate difference. The difference making brands may be those of highly desirable products – or they may be those of highly desirable and successful retail formats – "stores" if you will, physical or virtual.

In the UK, stores such as Marks & Spencer and Sainsbury successfully created their own brand names, which are often positioned as premium brands above or alongside national or global brands. Stores like Harrods

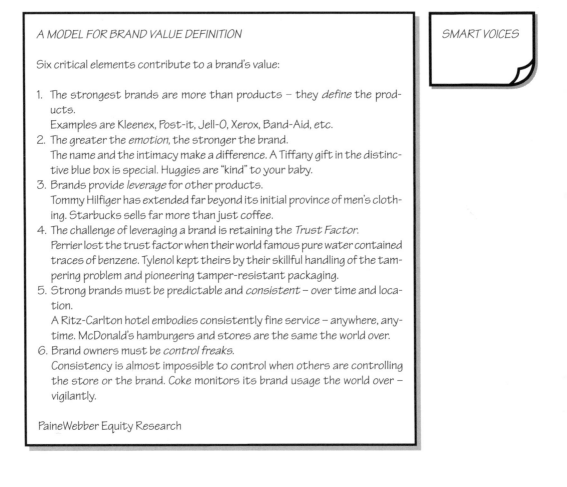

A MODEL FOR BRAND VALUE DEFINITION

Six critical elements contribute to a brand's value:

1. The strongest brands are more than products – they *define* the products.
   Examples are Kleenex, Post-it, Jell-O, Xerox, Band-Aid, etc.
2. The greater the *emotion*, the stronger the brand.
   The name and the intimacy make a difference. A Tiffany gift in the distinctive blue box is special. Huggies are "kind" to your baby.
3. Brands provide *leverage* for other products.
   Tommy Hilfiger has extended far beyond its initial province of men's clothing. Starbucks sells far more than just coffee.
4. The challenge of leveraging a brand is retaining the *Trust Factor*.
   Perrier lost the trust factor when their world famous pure water contained traces of benzene. Tylenol kept theirs by their skillful handling of the tampering problem and pioneering tamper-resistant packaging.
5. Strong brands must be predictable and *consistent* – over time and location.
   A Ritz-Carlton hotel embodies consistently fine service – anywhere, anytime. McDonald's hamburgers and stores are the same the world over.
6. Brand owners must be *control freaks*.
   Consistency is almost impossible to control when others are controlling the store or the brand. Coke monitors its brand usage the world over – vigilantly.

PaineWebber Equity Research

can use their store name as a cachet-carrying brand of its own. German discount grocer Aldi has kept much of its food offerings in its own exclusive brands, thereby gaining a level of control not available to other grocers. In the US, retailers like Home Depot now sell famous brands that are exclusively available at their stores.

As PaineWebber puts it in layman's terms – their stocks may be able to sell at higher prices or earnings-per-share (EPS) multiples! This can reduce their cost of capital and make it easier for them to make acquisitions or fund growth based on their stock value. All because of their "brand."

If these six elements are carefully managed, such as they are with Tiffany, GAP, Starbucks, etc., then some unique benefits can accrue to the brand. Carefully controlled or captive brands help ensure better, more consistent quality of the offering. Private labels and store brands can also do this more readily. Such well built and carefully controlled brands usually command premium pricing (and profits). It is hard to think of an enduring brand that built its name on the lowest price although the Internet model of giving things away free may alter that temporarily. Sooner or later, someone has to make a profit greater than the cost of capital to keep playing the game.

The chart below illustrates this principle quite graphically. The bottom line is that by concentrating on the six elements that define a strong brand, companies become both more effective/competitive in their markets with consumers and more attractive/valuable to investors.

The Market Share Of Brands

Brands Have Deeper Share Than Retailers

Product	Share	Retailer	Share
Microsoft	80%	Toys R Us	23%
Campbell's	60%	GNC	23%
Gillette	53%	Sunglass Hut	20%
Coke	46%	Home Depot	16%
Cascade	46%	Foot Locker	15%
Tide	43%	Wal*Mart	15%
Duracell	43%	Kroger	10%
Kellogg's	35%	Staples	6%

PaineWebber Equity Research April 13, 1999

Brands known globally are very valuable

Consumers care about brand names, and they vote with pictures of heads of state and dead presidents (money) for the brand they care most about. Brands help companies identify products and services in unique ways that differentiate them from competitors in the minds of consumers. Globalization increases a strong brand's importance when it can bridge language and cultural barriers.

The Nike swoosh is just as well known in Bremen, Germany; Beijing, China; or Boston, MA USA. Why? Because Nike makes the effort and spends the money on ads and endorsements to make the swoosh familiar around the world.

Smart quotes

Brands are very important to national cultures.

David Lightle, International brand consultant

Rubbermaid on the other hand is widely known and preferred for house-wares in the US market, but not nearly so well known around the world. The Curver name is better known and desirable in Europe, a fact that always irritated Rubbermaid management. Yet, their vaunted Rubbermaid brand name simply doesn't translate well in countries like the UK where it is met with smirks more often than smiles (because it is too easily associated with a rubber sex toy than with household storage containers).

Brands are even more important when brand differences are subtle

Titleist golf balls are known and used around the world because it has created a mystique that makes the product seem superior to competing products. Whether Titleist balls are actually that much better (or any better) is a point of heated competitive debate. No matter – the brand has been established as better, and as long as so many tournament-winning professionals continue to play and endorse the brand, its image will remain strong. This is one of the best examples of the power of a brand on what could easily become a hard-to-differentiate product. There will be more on brands in the sporting good industry later.

Brand campaigns

Memorable ad campaigns can establish a brand

Advertising campaigns that last for years can cement brand names into the minds of consumers. A couple of decades ago, actor Karl Malden made his still memorable ads for American Express, "Don't leave home without it!" As Burger King circles the globe, "have it your way" does too. Good slogans can reinforce brands and add relevance to them in consumers' minds. Service industries are often selling less tangible products and thus the power of branding is very important. An advertising campaign for

Wendy's hamburgers featuring an old lady named Clara Peller popularized the phrase "Where's the beef" so much that it has now become part of the slang vernacular.

McDonald's restaurants were hugely successful with their "You deserve a break today ..." ad theme because it appealed to their primary customers – busy working parents who wanted anything to give them a break from their daily time-stressed routine. I often wonder why they abandoned it, or why they don't bring it back.

The same could be said for "Coke – it's the real thing." Of course it is – and no-one can claim otherwise. They even have a secret formula for it. Why would any company walk away

KILLER QUESTIONS

How much should we be spending to create this brand (as a percentage of net sales)?

Q: What is the monetary value of brand names? Are companies valuing it on their balance sheets.

A: It is immense, and many companies are valuing their brand name with intangible assets on their balance sheets. *Financial World* and others publish estimated values – for example, here are some world brand leaders values as of a few years ago.

- Coke $39 billion
- Marlboro $38.7 billion
- IBM $ 7.1 – $17* billion
- Microsoft $11.7 billion
- Intel $ 9.7 billion

You can bet they are all much higher now!!

Financial World magazine: 1995 estimates
* Interbrand Schechter estimate: also in 1995

from a tag line that so clearly defined the essence of their brand? Coke was so much "the real thing" that even they failed when they tried to introduce the "New Coke". People wanted "the real thing", not some new different-tasting substitute. Many lessons are learned, but some are not so well learned from such experiences.

Brand misfires – what's wrong with this picture?

KILLER QUESTIONS

Can one brand be successful with a campaign very similar to one that failed for another similar brand? (Time will tell.)

Consider Coke's initial diet cola entry, Tab. It still has a very small but loyal following, but after reviewing Tab's lackluster sales performance, and the cost to advertise another brand, Coke decided to go back and do an obvious brand extension – Diet Coke, and then Caffeine-free Diet Coke both using the Coke brand name with great success. It makes one wonder what Pepsi is thinking when they abandon advertising for Diet Pepsi and spend a fortune to launch "One" (to signify only one calorie – which someone decided was more important than their best known brand name). Sounds like another Tab to me – but only time will tell.

On the other hand, 7Up tried brand extensions on what was too narrow a consumer franchise. They were successful as the "Un-cola." When they introduced Diet 7Up which survived, Cherry 7Up which is still around, but barely, and then Diet Cherry 7Up, they merely subdivided their market share across four related brands which were all forms of the "Un-cola." The result, more distribution expense, more inventory, advertising fragmentation, and no more sales. Brand extensions are fraught with peril, as we will discuss in a later chapter.

Smart managers learn from their mistakes and don't repeat them. Brilliant managers learn from others' mistakes too, but only the most courageous will reflect hard enough to understand all those mistakes and they become smarter because they do.

Brand slogans convey important reasons to use brands

Which airline do you prefer? A lot depends on actual experiences, but even more depends on your perception of their "brand's" performance relative to competing "brands". How you feel about them determines which you choose when you have a similar schedule and fare structure. United wanted to be "the friendly skies" because they hoped you would want to fly in their friendly skies. Delta said "we love to fly and it shows," in hopes that you would fly with them to see. The imagery created with their brand is hoped to be the "tie-breaker" when you choose an airline.

> Smart things to say about brands
>
> Emotion beats logic every time.

Should you use FedEx or UPS? Many people recall one brand from the advertising slogan: "FedEx – when it absolutely, positively has to be there." It depends on many factors, not the least of which is which one you believe will deliver the goods (literally and figuratively) better, faster, more reliably or more economically based on your needs. Usually one brand is used habitually; it becomes the brand of choice until there are several bad experiences with it. Many people now use the FedEx name as a verb: "FedEx it to me." Thus the terrific growth of FedEx, leaving UPS scrambling to expand their air parcel service to catch up. In brand image, UPS is reliable ground-based delivery, and FedEx is rapid air-based delivery. Both can try

Smart answers to tough questions

Q: How loyal are people to brands that satisfy them?
A: In a 1997 Roper-Starch survey, 54% of the respondents strongly agreed with the statement "Once I find a brand that satisfies me, I usually don't experiment with new ones."

to change that image, but initial images are firmly entrenched in consumers' minds.

Well-communicated brand advantages maintain leadership positions

Hertz car rental offers similar vehicles and prices to their competitors Avis, Budget, National, and so forth. How are they to differentiate their brand? Their commercials with the tag line "not exactly" are designed to do just that – create a brand image that is just enough better than competitors to bring you their way when you need a rental car. Hertz capitalized on their "#1-Gold" program with their "not exactly" campaign. Hertz had built the infrastructure – covered walkways and lighted signboards with renter's names on them.

The ads portray harried business travelers racing to their rental cars in rainstorms, trying to beat the competitors to an important customer presentation. One customer rents from Hertz, and stays out of the rain, gets to their cars faster and with less hassle – the other customer doesn't, and must answer his boss's questions about whether they will: 1. Stay dry, and out of the rain (not exactly), 2. Have their car ready and waiting nearby (not exactly), and 3. get to the important meeting on time

– ahead of competitors (not exactly!). The theme of the campaign is memorable; there's Hertz and there's "not exactly."

This is a multi-faceted appeal to business travelers' most important issues of speed, convenience, and comfort – since price was not believed to be a strong brand differentiator. Hertz locked their brand in the mind of their most frequent and lucrative customers – business travelers, with an image of being more convenient, faster, more comfortable, and thus have remained the rental car leader.

Brand premium

Premium brands can be more profitable

Brand-name products or services that are widely known and respected usually command price premiums which may (or may not) be justifiable based on their performance advantage over competing weaker or non-branded offerings. There is little doubt that these products built that brand premium over the years, usually by offering better function, higher quality, greater durability, more reliability, or at least a greater "cachet".

Mercedes-Benz autos have traditionally commanded a premium price for luxury, status, safety, comfort and performance – roughly in that order. The

Smart quotes

The "2–10" item is a term we coined during my days with Huffy Bicycles for an add-on, either in styling or accessories that cost $2 and would allow us to raise the price by $10. A powerful brand logo alone can do that – except the price might go up by $20 or more!

Steve Goubeaux (former VP, Sales & Marketing, Huffy Bicycles, now Partner, Visual Marketing Associates)

three pointed Mercedes star is so coveted that the hood ornaments are often stolen from the cars to be used as key chain ornaments by the less financially fortunate. Mercedes dealerships support the brand's cachet with luxury treatment of purchasers whose cars are in for service. This brand and the product it describes have allowed Daimler-Benz (now DaimlerChrysler) to be one of the most profitable automakers in the world. Where to separate the brand from the product is hard to tell, but the combination is a success.

Since many of the features, function, quality and so forth are designed in; often times the cost premium is not nearly as much as the price premium, so there is also greater profit in premium branded products.

Smart quotes

A leader has the vision and conviction that a dream can be achieved. He inspires the power and energy to get it done.

Ralph Lauren

If you will think a minute about knit shirts offered by Polo Ralph Lauren brand and a similar shirt offered by mail order merchant Land's End, you will see the power of a premium brand. Examine the shirts carefully and there is almost no perceptible difference in the fabric, construction, style, or functional value – except for the small embroidered polo player emblem on the Polo brand shirt. Colors may vary slightly as Polo will choose some more fashion-forward colors in additions to staples like white, navy, etc.

The Land's End shirt sells for around $25. The Polo sells for around $50. Do you think the brand is worth the difference? Millions of consumers say "yes." They vote with their money – they will pay extra for the visible brand identity of the Polo brand shirt.

Sony has long been recognized around the world as a premier producer and seller of electronic entertainment products. Sony, like Mercedes has created a premium brand based on a technology and feature advantage, represented by its brand image. Sony products are consistently higher priced than competition, but command that price based on a combination of actual features and perceived brand premium. The Sony brand and their "Trinitron" (a sub-brand) TV sets command a price premium over what are very similar appearing and near comparable performing brand names such as Panasonic, Magnavox/Philips, and a substantial premium over Korean brands like Sanyo and Samsung.

KILLER QUESTIONS

Where should we set pricing for this brand – premium, broad mainstream or promotional/low end?

The Sony name conveys similar meaning to buyers of computer monitors based on the same technology. Most of the internal electronics of the sets may be assembled with many of the same components, on the same assembly lines as competitive units in a production shop in Malaysia or California. The brand name promises something – Sony quality and performance. Is it better? Many consumers, once again, vote "yes" with their money.

Smart things to say about brands

When you and your brand are on top is the time to worry – there is only one way to go and that is *down*, unless you do the right things to keep it on top – and fast, before competition does!

Sometimes the brand premium is hard to get and keep

Rubbermaid is a widely known and admired producer of household storage products. During the 1980s, under the leadership of Stanley Gault, this small Ohio maker of rubber dustpans created a plethora of innovative housewares and household storage products. As they did this, each new product was introduced at a price premium to the inferior-performing or less aesthetically pleasing competitive products. As long as Rubbermaid kept the string of innovation going, the brand name commanded a premium price, even in discounters like Wal*Mart.

Unfortunately, in the mid 1990s, knock-off artists – companies who made "looks-like, works-like and costs-less" products copied Rubbermaid's best sellers and undercut their premium prices. Unlike Sony, Polo and Mercedes, the Rubbermaid brand was attached to such a mundane assortment of products that the price premium was not sustainable by the perceived quality or feature differences.

Today, Rubbermaid has been acquired by Newell. Newell did some things similarly to Rubbermaid in their kitchen, personal, office and hardware products but they did one major thing different – they paid much more attention to their cost competitive manufacturing and distribution competency. Thus, Newell was able to block the low price knock-off artists more

---

Smart answers to tough questions

Q: Building a brand is expensive and takes a long time – why not just lower prices?

A: In building a brand, you are building a long-term value position in the mind of consumers – and one that is lasting in nature – it is an investment in the future. Anybody can lower prices, and the last person with a sharp pencil wins – but just until a competitor with an even sharper pencil and lower price comes along.

effectively than Rubbermaid who had put all of their proverbial eggs into the product innovation basket.

The premium image

How do such brands build the image that gets them the premium price? Many different ways, but certainly with smart brand builders using advertising is the most prominent way. Sony probably makes a slightly better piece of equipment, and tests it to tougher standards, which result in a demonstrably better operating life, picture resolution, or preferred features. Polo creates visual images of the "beautiful people" wearing their clothing in settings that are enviable to the majority of their purchasers. Their message is, "You may not be able to actually have polo ponies or hang out at the polo club, but buy and wear our shirt, sweaters, or whatever and you can look just like the people who do. You will stand out from the crowd in ordinary settings. The insignia will mark you as a person of discriminating taste."

Have I embellished what the premium brand message says? Not a bit! People steal the hood ornament of their cars because the Mercedes-Benz three-pointed star is such a world-renowned symbol of status and quality. It has taken DaimlerBenz many decades to build their Mercedes brand name. Polo/Ralph Lauren is a somewhat more recent phenomenon, having been built in the last two decades.

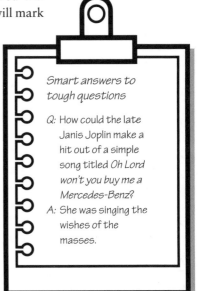

Smart answers to tough questions

Q: How could the late Janis Joplin make a hit out of a simple song titled *Oh Lord won't you buy me a Mercedes-Benz?*

A: She was singing the wishes of the masses.

Innovation adds value to a brand – unless it goes wrong

During an era in the 1980s and early 1990s, Benetton was considered a highly innovative retailer. Their colorful

Smart things
to say about
brands

"Pride goeth before the fall." Few things are more deadly than to fall so deeply in love with your own ideas that you are blinded to their flaw. Find a "truth-teller" to help you keep your perspective clear.

styles and shops full of designer sweaters and casual wear were very success-ful. Their advertising campaign "United Colors of Benetton" featured youth-ful multi-cultural models wearing their colorful fashion forward apparel. Then, in the interest of shock innovation, Benetton went over the edge, made some ads, which were risqué, in poor taste – mixing AIDS, sex, clergy and children – and some that others thought were borderline pornographic. The stores that had expanded so rapidly saw sales going flat and then de-clining. Imitators had knocked off the best styles, and the more radical ones went quickly out of style. Benetton, still a very large organization went from a hot brand name to an almost forgotten one – in a very short time frame – although it remains a large global company, its strength and brand franchise is diminished.

Innovation can create strong new sub-brands

Vlasic Foods International is a $1.4 billion pickle and frozen foods com-pany in the US. Pickles are not a particularly easy item to make into a differentiated brand, but still Vlasic is the supermarket brand-share leader. How can they innovate? The answer – make pickle slices that don't fall out of the sandwich. They started by slicing the cucumbers (from which pickles are made) length-wise. They coined a brand name for them "Stackers," which was memorable and described how these new cut pick-les were better. This made a longer flatter slice, but Vlasic was "in a pickle" of a dilemma. There is no way to patent the way you slice pickles, so competition could make these kind of slices too.

At this point Vlasic really innovated. It enlisted the help of their researchers to develop a strain of giant cucumbers – big enough across that a slice will cover an entire hamburger. Now "Stackers" have really arrived. The new brand name, which is very descriptive, and tells about not just a new way to slice pickles, but a new super-slice of pickle. The strong shelf placement of Vlasic accelerated the success of "Stackers" but, even without this strength, the marketplace seems to seek out and find innovative brands.

Brand value connotations are important

Before I leave this topic of a brand's benefits, I must discuss the issue of understanding value and how a brand contributes to the value perception. Value is a complex topic. Value is ever changing. It is situational. It is contextual. It actually exists in the eyes and mind of the customer, but is constantly being interpreted by the minds of the marketer. But value is also a constantly changing image in the consumer's mind.

There are physical attributes of value: Quality, Service, Speed, Cost, and Innovation. These can help describe value in terms everyone can relate to and agree upon. There are also higher levels of value – these are the consequences of the attributes and can lead to the fulfillment of perceived or unrealized higher order needs.

Gatorade, the famous "thirst quencher" portrayed in ads is a product of just such a value understanding. Gatorade undertook massive research into what exactly was important about their brand, and how to convey those messages and images to their current and potential users. The results were phenomenal.

Gatorade became *the* Thirst Quencher, although there were numerous imitators, some backed with big names and big money. Why? Because the marketers of Gatorade paid attention to the strategy, the brand's image and the brand's character while understanding what it was about the product that the customer really wanted, liked, and needed. They translated the brand's value into the brand's message. Success!!

The Rolls-Royce brand name is synonymous with super-premium luxury automobiles around the world. Owning it would be a real coup. Thus, when Rolls-Royce (the company) was put on the block by its investor–owners, it drew a lot of interest from two German companies. Volkswagen, who could use a really high end name to put above the Audi name and compete with Mercedes-Benz, and BMW. The bidding was intense as the two well-known companies tried to acquire Rolls-Royce.

> **Smart things to say about brands**
>
> When you really need something, you'll pay for it, whether you buy it or not. But if you do buy it, make sure you get what you paid for!

Then Volkswagen made a serious mistake as it spent $800 million to buy Rolls-Royce. The bidding with BMW was a heated affair, filled with back-and-forth bids, and bitter recriminations. VW won the bidding, but BMW got the last laugh. VW ended up with an old Rolls-Royce factory, and the Bentley name, but BMW scooped up the famed Rolls-Royce brand name for a fraction of the money. It seems the brand name and the company had two different owners. Who do you think is happier with that deal? The smart brand manager always makes sure who really owns the legitimate rights to the brand name before trying to buy the name. If you don't, you may end up with little or nothing valuable to show for your investment.

At times, a large part of the brand's success is the image the name creates in the mind, the brand cannot convey the wrong message or it becomes an undesirable name. In an era of global markets and brands, the name's meaning in other languages is very important. Exxon selected that name after learning that its earlier brand Esso had negative connotations in some countries/languages. Rubbermaid was a strong US brand, but led to smirks and giggles in the UK because of its connotation with "sex toys." Some

There are three tiers of brand values: first, "functional" values; second, "expressive" values; and third, "central" values. Functional values govern the performance of the product. Coke refreshes the drinker … Functional values do not differentiate the product from its rival since Pepsi also refreshes … Expressive values say less about the product and more about the consumer. Consumers buy … Apple computers because they appreciate their creative and human values. These values reflect and enhance the consumer's sense of him/herself and provide a key source of differentiation. However, it is central values which are the most enduring and go right to the core of the consumer's system of beliefs. Central values, at their purest, are embodied in religious, national, or political persuasions. Product brand values can command comparable power when they embody mass movements or cultural trends. Coke, for example, had great central values when it joined in with the 1960s' style fervour for love and peace in the theme song, *I'd like to teach the world to sing.*

The World's Greatest Brands (Interbrand)

years ago, Chevrolet had a strong brand-name auto, the Nova. Upon taking this brand into Eastern European markets, they were perplexed by its poor reception. The reason – in local languages, "No Va" meant "don't go" – not exactly the best brand image or identity for a car!

In my earlier experience, we used the brand name Grand Teton for a mountain bike, and in the US it was a good product name. It brought to mind the image of the scenic Wyoming mountains of the same name. Unfortunately, we discovered that trying to sell this bike in French-speaking Quebec, Canada or in France was an embarrassment. The literal translation of Grand Teton in French described the size of a woman's breasts! How embarrassing! A smart brand builder makes sure the brand name translates appropriately in different countries and languages.

The message conveyed by a name, a theme, a slogan or a brand's advertising and promotion campaign can have tremendous power that lasts for decades – if it is a good one. Bad ones, mercifully, die rather quickly!

4

Building a Brand

HOW ARE BRANDS BUILT INTO HIGHLY RECOGNIZABLE NAMES, HOW NEW BRANDS ARE CREATED AND LAUNCHED AND WHAT IS THE INFLUENCE OF THE INTERNET ON BRANDS?

Advertising, promotion, consistent presentation, wide distribution and large sales over long time periods are the major ingredients of brand building. The Internet is making possible entirely new and revolutionary shortcuts to the same results – faster than ever before. For brands to be of lasting value, their creation, launch and support must be done properly.

Quality problems can damage a brand almost beyond repair.

Building a brand

Anyone can build a brand, right? It's not all that complicated, is it? The answers are "No, *not everyone* can build a brand," and "No, it *is complicated if it is done right*!" It takes time, thought, money and more time, thought and money. Are you convinced yet? No? Then read on about the times it worked and when it didn't – and why!

This chapter will relate how brands can be built into readily recognizable household names associated with specific products or services. Just creating a brand is expensive, but unless it is built into something meaningful, the value of the brand is not very great and the money is wasted. Plus, careers are built or destroyed because of such successes and failures. (That could mean yours!)

Advertising, promotion, consistent presentation, wide distribution and large sales over long periods are the major ingredients of successful brand building. The Internet is making possible entirely new and revolutionary ways to accomplish the same results – faster than ever before, but the ingredients are not that different. It's just like the difference between regular pudding and the instant kind. When they are both done, they don't taste much

The decision maker must have an accurate and comprehensive model both to guide the information utilized in formation of strategy and that used to assess effectiveness. This becomes especially serious when it is realized that a naïve or overly simplistic model can lead to completely erroneous actions without the decision maker ever being aware of this fact.

Dr Roger Blackwell

different, but the process of getting there happens a lot faster, and the ingredients vary too.

Brand building

Brilliant brand building

Two stories about brand building illustrate how global brands can be built from nothing in a fairly short span of time. Haagen-Dazs ice cream and Swatch watches were brands that did not exist just twenty short years ago. Swatch created their brand in answer to a desperate situation for the Swiss watch-making community (SMH). After a large part of their mid-price market share had been taken by quartz/electronic Japanese made watches by Seiko, Citizen and others, SMH decided to build the Swatch brand as a fashion watch. Prior to this, Swiss made watches were either low-cost time-measurement devices (which the Japanese were attacking successfully) or high-cost heirloom/jewelry grade investments.

KILLER QUESTIONS

What positioning do we want for the brand – vs. competition, vs. our own brands, etc.?

SMH defined the Swatch as a low-cost watch of excel-lent Swiss quality, but with a stylish, fun, youthful, and trendy personality. The concept of a fashion watch, of which owners might purchase many different ones for different moods, styles, or occasions was as fresh and new as the Swatch designs. The brand was launched us-ing giant watches hung from buildings, outlandish publicity stunts and major event sponsorships.

While Hugo Boss sponsored participants in elitist events like the Porsche Racing Team to reinforce its image, Swatch supported events preferred by its target customers – Freestyle World Cup skiing, World Break-Dancing

> To build strong brands in this uncertain environment, US based companies would do well to study their counterparts in Europe. Because they were forced to, companies in Europe have long operated in a context that seems to mirror some to the harsher realities of the post mass-media era.
>
> Erich Joachimsthaler and David A. Aaker, *The Harvard Business Review*, January–February 1997

Championships, Alternative Miss-World Contests, and the like. New designs were often linked to specific events. Collecting unique Swatch watches became a popular trend. A customer membership club tied these efforts together into one of the most brilliant new brand launches of the past two decades.

The Haagen-Dazs launch, which started in 1989 was similarly effective and off-beat when compared with traditional advertising-backed product launches. The Haagen-Dazs brand was created by Grand Met to compete with a number of small but well-established European premium ice-cream makers such as Scholler in Germany, Movenpick in Switzerland and Sagit in Italy. In other European countries like the UK, private labels held over 40% share of the take-home ice-cream market.

Grand Met chose to position Haagen-Dazs above existing brands and set the price 30–40% higher than competitors. This sent a clear premium brand message, and helped to further fund the launch once it was moving. The brand image was all "premium" – thicker, creamier and more expensive; a sensual, self-indulgent treat for sophisticated adults who deserved something better. Instead of traditional advertising claiming this position and image, Grand Met opened luxury ice-cream stores – cafés – in key status locations. Special, segregated and Haagen-Dazs branded freezers appeared in food stores. Cultural event sponsorship reinforced their low key but highly personal ad campaign. The advertising theme, "The Ultimate in Personal Pleasure" simply reeked with sensual meanings.

Haagen-Dazs brand awareness in the UK hit 50% in a few months. European sales shot up to over $100 million in less than five years. Haagen-Dazs still commands the top position and price of premium ice creams even though there have been many copiers. Building a such powerful brand is both challenging and rewarding – and something that happens rarely.

Some companies like Swatch and Haagen-Dazs have chosen to develop brands without the help of advertising. The *Harvard Business Review article* "Building Brands without Mass Media" (January–February 1997) is a good reference for those who simply cannot spend a lot of money to advertise.

Another company that built its brand name without consumer mass-media advertising is Manco, Inc. of Cleveland, OH, USA. Manco has devoted its

---

Q: Is there a way to establish a brand without conventional advertising campaigns?
A: You bet there is – and an example says how very clearly.

Cadbury links the brand to the experience.

Cadbury World "theme park" has served to reinforce the brand image and identity of Cadbury's centuries-old chocolate products better than any advertising campaign could have. Opened in 1990 at a cost of just under £6 million, the park brought hundreds of thousands of visitors opportunities to sample the famous line of chocolates. Attendance has approached 500,000 per year, and additional world-wide press coverage has help further enhance their famous brand name. Cadbury was named the most admired company in the UK in 1996, and there is no doubt that the creation of Cadbury World played a part in gaining that honor.

Smart answers to tough questions

resources to customer friendly services like 800 help lines, public relations events featuring their human-size fuzzy yellow duck and creative merchandising of its products – Duck® brand duct tape, masking tape, carton sealing tape, and CareMail® brand mailing supplies among many others.

Manco recently was acquired by Henkel KGaA, the multi-billion dM German company and is now in the process of adding advertising to its brand development mix. This story is a good illustration of how to develop a global brand from a smaller, less glamorous local brand. Henkel's $2.5 billion adhesive division makes it the world leader in this category. This, when combined with Manco's top tape brands and other leading consumer and office products, provides The Duck with global distribution. Through major advertising campaigns, the "Duck®" brand became a US-wide and is planned to become a world-wide leading brand for the combined tape and related products sold by Manco as part of Henkel.

Branding "The Duck"

The first step in building any brand is to find out what consumers know about the brand, and what they think it stands for – if anything. Unless you know where you are, how will you know the path to take to where you want to go? Thus Manco began with research on what consumers in the US knew about The Duck, and what they thought about it (research professionally undertaken – remember – this is not the place for amateur night!).

Much to their delight, research showed that The Duck, while not particularly well-known, was very well perceived. That is a great start for a brand-building campaign – at least there is no need to change people's image of the brand. The Duck was perceived as:

- imaginative

- resourceful

- helpful

- friendly

- fun.

Remember the importance of brands being friendly and fun. The Duck was felt to be "life's little helper!" Because of this, they selected the advertising tag line, "Get the duck to do it."

With this knowledge of how consumers perceived The Duck, Manco's advertising and marketing staff could decide how to position The Duck as a brand. One critical aspect of this was using The Duck in a consistent way that makes all of their related products a part of The Duck's friendly, helpful family. This was a challenge since products spanned home, office, and do-it-yourself (DIY) categories like tapes, adhesives, weather-stripping, caulking and more.

Their term for this campaign was even in keeping with its overall fun and friendly demeanor – Manco planned to "Duckify!" its products, its packaging, and in fact, its entire marketing efforts and the whole company. "Duckification Days" involved having employees wear Duckified apparel. Creating a culture within the company was an important aspect of carrying The Duck's helpful, friendly nature to their customers around the world.

THE HERITAGE OF THE DUCK

Manco began as the Melvin A. Anderson Company in 1950, serving Cleveland's strong and heavily industrialized markets with pressure-sensitive tape. Pressure-sensitive tape technology has been the core business from which all Manco businesses have evolved. In 1971, after selling tape for the Melvin A. Anderson Company, Jack Kahl purchased the company, renamed it Manco, Inc.

The company alternately struggled and then prospered as the demand for these products grew. As Jack shifted the company's focus from industrial sales to retail sales, he succeeded in selling to a small Arkansas retailer who has grown into the largest retailer in the world and Manco's largest customer – Wal*Mart. In this process, Jack Kahl was befriended by Wal*Mart founder Sam Walton, a friendship and mentorship that lasted for years, until Sam's death. Jack continued to invest in the business and expand Manco's retail distribution, in competition with powerhouse 3M, successfully using many of the principles he learned from Sam Walton and Wal*Mart's growth. After hearing customers repeatedly refer to duct tape as "duck tape," Jack seized on the idea of naming it "Duck Tape." Thus, The Duck was born as a cute, cuddly little character wearing the Manco colors and sash.

During the 1978 energy crisis, Manco's bright-green packaging created the "Sea of Green" retail look of household tapes and weather-stripping which was an instant retail success. During the decade of the 1980s, Manco's fortunes ebbed and then grew as the company matured. Jack's two sons, John and Bill joined their father in the company after their graduation from college, and took active roles in the sales organization.

By the mid 1990s, Manco had created whole new merchandise categories like CareMail™ mailing supplies, and rivaled or exceeded 3M in market share for tapes sold through major mass market retailers. The Manco name and its cuddly Duck icon had grown in stature in retail channels of distribution as additional new product offerings were being developed and introduced rapidly.

The Duck has been pictured wearing mail carrier's outfits, and painter's caps to mirror Manco's mailing and DIY product ranges, but through it all, The Duck has remained smiling – cute, cuddly, fun and friendly. Manco partners (their name for employees since the company was an ESOP – Employee Stock Ownership Partnership) dress up in life-sized Duck costumes to appear as goodwill ambassadors at trade shows, retail store openings, and charitable events.

Like all of Manco's businesses, the Home Solutions™ business category was born of listening to customers at the 1994 Housewares Show. Easy Liner® brand shelf liner was test marketed and launched, launching Manco into a whole new market segment. Home Solutions™ and Softex™ products have grown into major sub-brands that center around kitchen and bath housewares and provide new, imaginative, value added solutions for the home.

In 1998, Henkel KgaA, $12 billion German company purchased Manco, Inc. and is intensely pursuing branding The Duck around the world.

Objectives were developed and guidelines created for Duckification. Existing products presented challenges in naming and packaging interpretations. Henkel's existing product brands – Pritt, Loctite and LePage had to be rationalized with The Duck as to which brand fit which of the products and markets. This is a classic case of brand management in application.

Package and merchandising revisions were studied carefully to find where The Duck's appeal fitted best and how to extend the logo of The Duck without over-reaching its appeal and target audience of consumers. Manco advertising VP Gary Medalis led an effort to create a family of "Duck" TV advertising and print media campaigns using animated "Get the Duck to do it" tags were developed. Print campaigns paralleled the use of the "Get the Duck to do it" tag line for continuity. The message was elegant in its simplicity. The Manco "Duck" brand products were all about being

Manco identified seven areas that needed to be "Duckified" as part of their "branding The Duck" campaign:

- corporate identification and image
- merchandising materials (internal)
- merchandising packaging (external)
- trade show materials & booths
- collateral materials
- apparel and gift items
- public relations.

Gary Medalis (VP, Advertising and Communications, Manco Inc.)

helpful in tasks – large and small – that happen everyday. Time-starved consumers can accomplish these tasks easily by simply remembering to "Get the Duck to do it"

Packaging was re-done to feature the duck in its proper place to prominently remind purchasers of this trustworthy and helpful little character's role: "Get the Duck to do it."

An e-commerce campaign based on Manco's web site (www.Manco.com) is being developed to further expand The Duck's reach and brand awareness. At this writing, The Duck is already evident in the UK, and by the year 2000, is making its European (Henkel's home market) debut in Germany, Italy, France, Benelux, Spain, Poland, Hungary, the Czech Republic, Slovakia. Turkey (and around the world in Australia, New Zealand, and the Philippines). Wal*Mart, Manco's largest customer is taking The Duck with them as they go global – to Canada and Mexico, to South America (Brazil and Argentina), and even to China. This is clearly a busy little Duck!

What is the most challenging part of building a global brand? Within each country or each marketing area, there are different ideas, philosophies, and cultures. Trying to get those different people to agree on what the brand stands for is very difficult – that is the most challenging part of building a global brand.

Bill Kahl (Executive VP, Manco, Inc.)

A global brand product launch of this nature is only possible because of the homework done by Manco's Global SBU under the leadership of Bill Kahl, with the support of Henkel's existing global distribution network. Once the Duck is a global brand, the presence of such consumer-friendly features and the Internet based Duck Tape club will further enhance the brand's image and salience with consumers.

Manco's Duck-brand launch will use its corporate Internet web site *www.Manco.com*, (and don't be surprised if the name becomes *www.duck.com* by the time this is published) to launch the Duck Tape Club – a partly serious, partly fun and entertaining mixture of ways to use Duck tape, both real and imagined. Some of these applications will come, no doubt from the uses shown on the limited exposure but wild and wacky US cable TV show, "The Red Green Show" and from Manco's touring Duck tape ambassadors. From frivolous fun-loving uses to serious do-it-yourself tips for the uses of tape and adhesive products, the internet can provide a new, interactive way for Henkel-owned Manco to launch a global club, and connect to club members anywhere, anytime, about anything.

The "Club" forms a community of consumers

Several companies have used clubs of owners to build and reinforce the community of brand-loyal followers. The most notable of these is the

<table>
<tr><td>

Smart quotes

</td><td>

In developing the plan for a global brand, two things are critical for success: 1) Make sure the structure is set up properly; 2) In that structure, be sure the people with the responsibility and accountability also have the authority needed to execute the plan.

Bill Kahl

</td></tr>
</table>

Harley-Davidson Harley Owners Group (HOG) which coincidentally corresponds to the nickname many people give to their Harley-Davidson motorcycles. Meetings, huge rallies and common apparel are just a few of the elements that build a community of fiercely brand loyal customers.

Another is the Casa Buitoni Club, which Nestlé used to build interest and usage of their pasta products. The 169-year-old Italian pasta company was able to dramatically increase its brand awareness and sales through its 1993 launch of the Casa Buitoni Club and its advertising campaign theme of "Share the Love of Italian Food". Members receive recipes, discount vouchers, toll-free advice lines, and more.

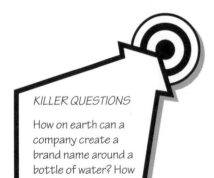

KILLER QUESTIONS

How on earth can a company create a brand name around a bottle of water? How did Perrier, Evian and others do it?

Brands can be built many ways

The most common way to build a brand is advertising and promotion combined. Take a new brand such as the drinking-water brand being introduced by Coke, named Dasani. Water is one of the earth's most common resources.

Perrier and Evian created brand names for water in a bottle. They created brands that were status symbols. Perrier was a fashionable, low-in-calories, socially acceptable alternative to an alcoholic cocktail. Evian did it with water from the French Alps! Amazing. US airline companies on the verge of bankruptcy were hauling water from the French Alps in small bottles over to the US and then loading it on their planes to serve to thirsty (but status conscious) travelers.

A *well-built brand is a powerful thing!*

Pepsi has its own brand of bottled water – Aquafina, and soon Coke will have its Dasani brand. Such names were carefully chosen to have subtle meanings and to sound like something more than they are – a bottle of purified tap water – just like you drink at home, but packaged and delivered in a way that makes it convenient to take with you (something you could do by filtering your tap water!).

A smart brand builder never forgets the power of distribution in building a brand. The massive power of Coke's distribution system will help launch Dasani. In 1998 consumers spent $4.2 billion on plain bottled water, and that market is growing as health-conscious consumers choose water or various artificial fruit juices. Do the names Snapple and Fruitopia sound familiar? These are the new recreational drink, instead of carbonated, sweetened and preservative laden soft drinks.

Thus it is only logical that Coke and Pepsi, the two largest mainstream beverage companies want their own brands of bottled water, and with their clout in distribution, they will have them.

Building brands means having memorable names or icons

Sometimes brands are built upon the premise of an unlikely name. J.M. Smucker Co. is a leading producer of jams and jellies. They decided to

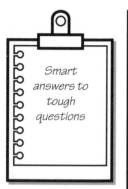

Q: How is a brand built?

A: Simply (not easily – just simply) in three major ways – Distribution, Promotion and Advertising

Consumers can't buy it if they can't find it!

Distribution – prominent mass displays in supermarkets, drug stores, convenient stores, airports, mass retail outlets of all kinds present the face of the brand to millions of potential buyers. Companies will pay slotting allowances, buy back competitors' products and provide all of the display fixtures and signage at no cost to get precious premium retail shelf/floor space.

Give the consumer a reason to try your new brand!

Promotion – Sunday papers will carry cents-off coupons, salty snacks (of course!) and other products will do tie-in promotions, retailers will gladly accept money for prominently placed special displays and placards. Free giveaways at supermarkets, entertainment events, and sporting events to kick off the campaign and to launch the brand. PR campaigns can even be launched to emphasize the importance of using the new product.

Make sure consumers know you brand is out there and what it stands for

Advertising – somehow a message is crafted to present the brand with a brand character and image that makes it desirable, something like "new", "light", "fresh," "pure" (yes, *really!* – never underestimate the need for consumers to be reminded of the most obvious things!). The media approach will be the obvious: TV, especially on popular, trendy shows, key sporting events, selected print media, talk radio, even on the Internet! Beautiful people will be seen using the product, and consumers will (hopefully) imagine that if they use it they will be like the beautiful people.

make the unusual corporate name the centerpiece of their brand building campaign. "With a name like Smuckers, it's got to be good!" was their theme. And it worked. Smuckers is now a widely recognized and accepted premium brand for supermarket jams and jellies.

Heinz ketchup used a different memorability factor – the distinctive shape of their bottle, the thickness of the product (not watery like cheap ketchups) and widespread distribution to fine restaurants and dining establishments. For a long time my wife, sold on Heinz Ketchup quality by using it at home, assigned a perception of additional quality to eating establishments who used Heinz Ketchup – in its own distinctive bottle – instead of generic containers which had who-knows-what kind of possibly watered-down ketchup (or catsup) in them. Heinz then employed TV adds to reinforce that their ketchup was thick, not watered down. The ads showed a person waiting for the (thick) Heinz ketchup to come out of the distinctive bottle. The brand was built upon these images all the way from distribution to promotion and advertising.

Brand advertising

Smart things to know about advertising lingo

Advertising is a critical element of creating and supporting brands. That makes it an important topic, and one worthy of your understanding. When speaking about advertising with ad executives, you can easily to get caught in a conversation with a set of terms that are completely unfamiliar. Ad people will talk about rating points, reach, frequency, SOA, SOV, SOM, and so forth. What does this all mean? What follows is a simplified primer on advertising terminology for smart brand builders to help you break through the confusion and misunderstandings. It is really important for you to know these things, because an advertising agency or media-buying firm might make promises, take your money and deliver on the promises when the result was far from what your brand needed!

Target Market

The target market is the audience you have identified that you want the ads for your brand and product or service to reach. These are often described in one of many ways:

- age demographic terms, such as ages 13–25, or other age categories broken down by homogeneous market segments or to match census data often used for analysis.

- gender: male or female.

KILLER QUESTIONS

- Who is our target market and how much of it will we reach with our brand and this advertising campaign?
- What will the reach and frequency of the campaign be, and at what cost per million (CPM) impressions?

- minorities (US basis) – African-American (blacks, typically), Hispanic (usually means an origin/descent from Spanish speaking countries), Asian, etc.

- job, career or profession: working mothers, two-income families, white-collar or blue-collar.

- geo-political areas such as cities, states, provinces, counties, or other defined boundaries (a common term used in advertising is SMSA – Standard Metropolitan Statistical Area – the area surrounding a major city and measured/influenced by its media/advertising).

- other breaks that might be specified such as parents of children in specific age groups, household income levels, special interest groups, retirees, etc.

These target markets are most often reached by advertising in/on specific media. Women might be reached by cable networks or sites on the Internet, which may advertise themselves as the network or site for women, or magazines like *Women's Day*, *Vogue*, *Glamour*, – again depending on the age, income, profession, etc. Most media sellers of advertising publish the specific demographics of who they reach in these terms. Make sure you know how your brand is being advertised and to whom – otherwise you might end up advertising skateboards or in-line skates to senior citizens or Viagra to the under-13 age group – clearly a waste of the money on that advertising target.

Rating Points

This is a measure of "reach" – how many of the audience sees or hears the ads and "frequency" – how many times this part of the audience is reached by an ad during a specified time period. For example, in a one-week "flight" of ads, aimed at the entire population from ages 16 and up (such as an institutional ad for a car company) an ad that is seen by 50% of the population has a "reach" of 50. If this ad is seen an average of 3 times by those who see it, it has a frequency of 3. The rating points calculation is 50 (reach) times 3 (frequency) or 150 rating points in this one-week flight of ads. Advertisers refer to flights in describing a particular set of ads over a specific time period a strategic or tactical marketing or brand development purpose in mind. Obviously ads have different life cycles. Internet ads may stay in place for days or hours. Magazines may linger on tables for days or weeks. TV ads are run and gone in 30 to 60 seconds.

Beware of advertising people who talk of *Gross Rating Points* (GRPs) and not of Target Rating points. Gross rating points are measured by how many people of the general population in total saw the ad and how many times on average they saw it. This may have little to do with your brand's target market, especially if it is a small fraction of the total population. Get the ad execs to talk in terms of *Target Rating Points* (TRPs) – how many of your defined target saw the ads how many times during the time frame specified. That is what matters.

Another important advertising factor is the cost per thousand impressions. Advertising is communications. The less it costs to "reach" a lot of people, the more attractive it should be, but not always. This cost varies considerably for different advertising media because of the quality of the impressions and the nature of the audience being reached. This is why network television advertising costs have not dropped as much as expected from the influx of cable TV.

The popular youth demographic in the 18–35 age group still watches a lot

Q: What do those SOA, SOV, SOM terms mean anyway?
A: They are abbreviations for "share of" terms …

SOA – Share of Advertising is the actual measured share of advertising dollars spent for competing products going after the same product/service consumers in the same media markets. In simple terms, what share of the ad media spending was yours.

SOV – Share of Voice is the measure of viewership shares as a result of a longer-term campaign; in other words, how much of the "voice" of all the advertising run against that product/service and market did your advertising get?

SOM – Share of Market is the bottom line, based on actual sales outcomes. In simplest terms, who sold what percentage of a given category of product/service in a specified market segment over a specified time frame. This is what most advertisers want to achieve, because this is where money is made; both other measures are just how much is being spent for how much relative "noise" it makes.

of network programming. They cost more money to reach because advertisers badly want to reach them. Similarly, the cost of ads in magazines and publications that are sold cheaply, given away, or considered to be of low quality may be quite attractive – until consideration is given to the quality of the advertising impression made – then the price is appropriate.

Failure to understand these basics about advertising of brands is what causes large wasted expenditures for advertising that does little to build a brand or sell a product. Another key question to ask is whether the advertising's intent is to sell products directly (like

KILLER QUESTIONS

What forms of advertising and promotion will we use to launch and then support the brand?

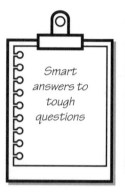

Smart answers to tough questions

Q: What are the most important issues in advertising to build brands?

A: There are two of them that stand above all the others:

1. Make sure your advertising campaign is reaching the audience you want to know about your brand, and that it is an audience that is likely to buy your product or service.

2. Make sure the quality of the ad, the image of the message and the choice of media matches those features of your brand.

infomercials do), to tie into retail promotions (like supermarkets often do) or to build brand recognition, recall, awareness, preference and loyalty over a long time frame. This objective makes a big difference in how the brand is portrayed in the advertising, and what the expected return on the brand development spending might be.

KILLER QUESTIONS

If we are successful, what kind of value will the brand add and how will we realize returns on our investments?

Enormous sums of money are spent to advertise and build brands

The table below shows only the spending for one-half of a year (1997)! Depending on which kind of promotions they use, and the money spent for slotting allowance (fees paid to supermarkets to secure shelf space), and floor planning (financing allowances given to car dealers to hold their inventory of new cars) those figures would easily exceed the advertising spending. Clearly, having a frequent prominent place for your product and brand in the mind of the consumer is a smart thing to do.

Name	Million $ spent
1. Chevrolet/GM (cars & trucks)	$321
2. McDonald's (restaurants)	$289
3. Ford (cars & trucks)	$287
4. Sears (retail stores)	$267
5. Dodge/Chrysler (cars & trucks)	$264
6. AT&T (phone services)	$250
7. MCI (phone services)	$213
8. Burger King (restaurants)	$197
9. Toyota (cars & trucks)	$188
10. Kellogg's (breakfast foods)	$172

Advertising Age web site archives (www.adage.com)

Building a brand around some desirable characteristic

Maytag Corporation, a large US manufacturer of laundry equipment and other major appliances built their brand upon legendary quality and reliability. Their advertising theme was "The Maytag repairman – the loneliest man in the world." Gordon Jump, a self-effacing, middle-aged character actor portrays the forlorn and forgotten Maytag repairman superbly. The machines are so reliable the poor man has nothing to do – and you (and I) the consumers remember that reliability and pay handsome premiums to Maytag for their appliances.

M&M candy built a major advertising campaign and the basis for their brand on the characteristic that they were a chocolate candy that did not melt in your hand. There were many chocolate candies in the market place, but how to differentiate this brand from them was an issue. While children are large candy consumers, parents are more concerned about avoiding chocolate stains on the kids clothing. This benefit became a good theme to appeal to parents who purchase the candy for their kids. Making the hard sugar-coating multi-colored made the brand more "fun" for kids and this was also a major contributor to its success. But the single theme: "melts in your mouth, not in your hand" was the key. Later many other candies, including arch rival Hershey's Reese's Pieces would emulate M&M's hard, melt-resistant, colorful coating, but M&M has already staked out that brand position in the consumer's mind.

Building a brand for a "part that is greater than the whole"

Intel Corporation made what was a largely undifferentiated component of a personal computer a highly recognized brand name. The "Intel Inside" brand campaign was launched using all three of the major brand building methods: distribution, promotion, and advertising. Until then, consumers knew there must be some kind of processor chip inside their computers, but knew little and cared less about what kind of processor chip their computer contained. Intel usurped at least part of the brand differentiation from computer makers and transferred it to "Intel Inside" processor chips.

The "Intel Inside" logo appeared on products, initially supported with some form of chip discounts from Intel, and then as the brand grew, a premium was demanded by Intel in return for early availability of each succeeding new generation of processor chip! As Intel's success grew, they plowed more money into advertising to convince consumers that their chips were better, faster, and somehow superior to competitors.

Whether Intel's chips were better or not matters little, because consumers accepted the premise and were willing to look for, ask for and pay a premium for PCs with Intel processors. With PC makers' help, Intel cleverly camouflaged exactly what the premium cost was: there were simply too many other variables in computer specifications to single out and identify the premium for the Intel Pentium processors (their most popular sub-brand).

A similar strategy for building a component brand name, which transcended the product brand, was used by Shimano in bicycle components. Shimano was a highly automated Japanese manufacturer of bicycle brakes, derailleur gear shifting systems and other parts of the bicycle drive train – hubs, cranks, sprockets, etc.

The primary sources of components in the bicycle market shifted from Europe in the 1970s to Japan in the 1980s and then to Taiwan, Korea, Malaysia and China in the 1990s. Shimano concentrated on refining its design of high-performance components and the automated factories to make them at very competitive costs with superb quality.

By the early 1990s, Shimano was not only the innovative leader in this field but was "bundling" components into "groups," a practice originated in Europe in earlier decades, by Campagnolo the long-time leader in racing components. The rationale was that a group of components worked best together and Shimano took the responsibility for a large part of the "systems integration" instead of the bike manufacturer. What a clever trap Shimano had set. The entire bike industry walked in, and just as PC makers did with Intel a decade later in computer processor chips, Shimano essentially took over control of the major differentiators for these products.

The bike manufacturers could change the shape of frames and forks and hang other cosmetic items on to differentiate themselves, just as PC makers can change cases, displays/monitors and memory content, but ultimately Shimano and Intel have stolen the heart of the product with their brands. Bikes were described as having Shimano XYZ group and that set their relative price and prestige in the product market hierarchy, just as Intel's 286, 386, 486 and then Pentium, Pentium II, MMX, Pentium III, claimed top brand billing in its computer industry.

Private labels & store brands

Store brands are a force to be reckoned with

A phenomenon that seems to ebb and flow with economic cycles is the

Smart quotes

> Forward-thinking retailers will transform not just their lines but their entire stores into brands in the minds of consumers. The goal? Getting consumers to buy "the store" and not just the national or store brands it carries.
>
> Dr Roger Blackwell

creation of store brand – often called private labels since they are usually limited to the use of the retailer or its parent company. One of the most famous users of these store brands is Sears. Sears built their Kenmore appliance and Craftsman tool product brands into highly known and respected names. In the heyday of Sears, Roebuck & Co.'s other two national competitors, JCPenney and Montgomery Ward, their private brands were also well known. In sporting goods, the names J.C. Higgins (Penney) and Hawthorne (Wards) were often found in their stores in much greater numbers than national brands like Wilson, Spalding and others. As Wal*Mart surpassed all other retailers in size and competence, they too have developed "store brands" or private labels such as Old Roy (pet foods), Sam's American Choice (food and drink), and Popular Mechanics (hardware). Wal*Mart's sheer size and retailing clout alone will make these brands large sellers. Remember the part about distribution being a critical element of brand success?

Private-label grocery products were originated in the US by the grocery chain, the Great Atlantic and Pacific Tea Company, (now just called A&P), and the company still markets its own store-brand products under the America's Choice brand. Private-label grocery products have made progress against national brands, and now claim 10–15 percent of overall supermarket spending.

There are big product-based differences in what drives consumer demand for private brands versus national brands. Some analysts contend that store brands can grow by filling in gaps that national brands leave on supermarket shelves, but more likely private labels will grow at lower price levels or

Every decade or so, the wise gurus proclaim either name brands or private brands to be dead or dying. Such is seldom the case. There is a place and a reason for both, and thus both will survive indefinitely.

Smart things to say about brands

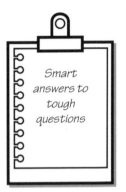

Q: Are there ways to characterize consumers that help clarify the targets for certain kinds of brands and branding.

A: Yes, in advanced retail information environments, this kind of information is available. Below is an example of some US consumer profiles.

Heavy buyers
- Spent an average of $660 on store brand goods during the year, compared with about $5,400 for all consumer packaged goods.
- Live in a family with an annual household income between $20,000 and $40,000.
- Are likely to be blue-collar workers with household heads are typically aged 35–44, high-school educated.
- Families often contain five or more members.
- Make up only 17 percent of all shoppers but account for 42 percent of spending on private-label products.

Occasional buyers
- Spend an average of $260 a year on private labels, compared with $3,800 a year on all packaged goods.
- Live in a family with an annual household income of $30,000 to $60,000.
- Household head is likely to be aged 45 to 64, high school-educated, and working part-time or retired. Many are/were also blue-collar workers.
- Family typically contains three or four members, which partly explains why they spend less than Heavy Buyers on packaged goods.
- Make up 44 percent of shoppers, and account for 44 percent of spending on private-label products.

Infrequent buyers
- Spend less than $90 on private-label products versus almost $2,800 on all items.
- Have a split personality; the head of household is most likely to be under age 35 or over age 65, and annual household income is likely to be either under $12,000 or over $60,000.
- Are professionals or white-collar workers with full-time jobs and college experience.
- Households are smaller, frequently containing only one or two members.

- Make up 39 percent of all shoppers, yet account for only 14 percent of spending on private-label products.

Location (US data only) characteristics vary as well!
- Southern and western states account for the largest shares of private-label buyers in every category.
- The South contains less than 35 percent of US residents, but is home to 40 percent of heavy private-label shoppers, 37 percent of occasional shoppers, and 30 percent of infrequent shoppers.
- About 25 percent of Heavy Buyers are from the western states, although this region contains 20 percent of the population as a whole.
- About 20 percent of Occasional Buyers and 19 percent of Infrequent Buyers are also from the West.
- The eastern states account for slightly more than 20 percent of the country's population and 19 percent of Heavy Buyers.
- The East also contains 20 percent of Occasional Buyers and 22 percent of Infrequent Buyers.
- Shoppers in the Midwest are the least enamored of private labels. The Midwest contains a quarter of the nation's population, and it accounts for only 16 percent of Heavy Buyers, 24 percent of Occasional Buyers, and 28 percent of Infrequent Buyers.

Minorities (US only)
- Hispanics are more likely than average to be Heavy Buyers. While they are less than 7 percent of the Nielsen household panel, they account for more than 8 percent of heavy private-label purchasers. They make up 7 percent of occasional purchasers and 6 percent of infrequent purchasers.
- Blacks represent a smaller share of Heavy Buyers. They are 11 percent of the Nielsen household panel, but less than 7 percent of heavy private-label buyers, 10 percent of occasional purchasers, and 14 percent of infrequent purchasers.
- Asian Americans account for 0.8 percent of the Nielsen household panel, 0.1 percent of heavy private-label purchasers, 0.3 percent of occasional buyers, and 1.5 percent of infrequent buyers.

Marcia Mogelonsky, "When Stores Become Brands," *American Demographics* magazine

in areas where national brands do dumb things that blur, fragment or destroy their brand image.

The pendulum swings toward and away from private label products every decade or so, often driven by economic cycles. In the 1950s and 1960s, TV advertising propped up national brands. In the 1970s and again in the 1980s private brands made progress as the economic climate pushed consumers toward low cost, high value products. As retailers such as the Wal*Mart and grocers Kroger and Aldi push their own brands at much lower prices for apparently comparable products, the pendulum will continue to swing. When the retailers are trusted and offer exchange of money back guarantees, the consumer is often willing to try the cheaper private label item instead of the branded alternative. It is then that the product's performance becomes the determining factor in consumer satisfaction and future brand choices.

In other situations, the store brand is the premium brand. Marks and Spencer, for example, place some of their store brands at prices comparable to or higher than major branded products. Nordstrom does the same with certain of their private label items. Cases like this show that store names can carry brands even against entrenched, advertised competition.

Creating new brands or fixing old ones

Volkswagen had a huge success in the 1960s, the Beetle. This small car became an icon of the era. Similar models are still built in the VW Mexican plant, but are not qualified to meet US emission and bumper standards, so they require expensive modifications to be sold in the US.

VW also created a minivan before anyone else. It was the vehicle of choice for the "flower-children" of its era. The sales of the "Beetle" and the "Minibus" made Volkswagen bold. The third member of the family, the Kharmann

Ghia is still a collector's item. VW was already a leader in broad segments of the auto market in Europe. This was a case where their brand image in the two markets was widely different.

Then VW did a really dumb thing. They decided to replace the Beetle, and discontinue the Mini-bus and Kharmann Ghia. Perhaps refitting them to meet US developing standards for safety and emissions would have been too expensive. That is not the point. VW had a brand image in this country. They made and sold small cars and vans that were fun, whimsical, and unique. They owned that market segment in the minds of consumers. Perhaps the fact that VW senior management and corporate culture was European led to their misunderstanding of the unique market position and image they had in the US. In any case, whatever the reason, VW blew it!

After huge successes in the tough US market, what did VW do? They gave away their consumer franchise! VW made a serious, stodgy small car and a dull, un-interesting larger car, and totally destroyed the image of its brand in its segment. Of course they tried to give the small car a "cute" name – the Rabbit – but to no avail. After this move met with little success, they decided to return to the car's European name, the Golf, and making it sporty by creating a GTI version.

No luck. To Americans, golf is a game, not the name of a car! By not developing a replacement for the Beetle that resembled it (which they took about two decades to do and is a big success ... even now!) VW showed that they didn't understand their brand's character and image in the US. VW management may not have wanted its brand image to be what it was, considering their corporate ego as a large European car company. VW may not have wanted to be the company that makes these silly little vehicles that sell so well to flaky Americans, but consumers make those decisions, not corporate management, and American consumers had voted for the old VW products with their money. When the Beetle, the Mini-Bus and

Fixing a damaged brand is difficult and not always successful – make sure it is worth the effort. Only if the brand that is "fixed" is a very strong one, do the cost and time to "repair" it (and the risk of failure) make sense.

the Kharmann Ghia went away, those brand icons went away too. The bottom line was, this virtually destroyed the VW brand in the US for a couple of decades.

Dealing with a damaged brand is difficult

In the 1980s VW had established the Audi 5000 as a fine, mid-level luxury sedan in the US market. The VW brand continued to suffer with the lackluster Golf and Passat models, but consumers did not connect VW and Audi. Then brand disaster lightning struck VW a second time.

Audi's very successful model 5000 was accused of having a design flaw that caused a sudden acceleration to occur when moving the foot from the brake to the accelerator just after starting the car. Accident reports flowed in from many places and they detailed major injuries resulting from this alleged defect. After months of controversy, testing proved that the sudden acceleration problem was a myth, not a genuine defect in the car. Perhaps the positioning and shape of the brake and accelerator pedals confused drivers, or were too close by some expert opinions, but it was determined that the sudden acceleration was essentially driver error.

Unfortunately, while this debate raged on, the Audi 5000's value dropped like a rock. The brand's quality and safety image had been all but destroyed. As a result of this debacle, all of today's autos have a shift lock which assures the driver's foot is firmly on the brake when the car is shifted from park to either reverse or drive – eliminating the risk of sudden acceleration entirely.

Well defined brands send a single powerful message to customers and employees alike. There are three steps to creating such a brand statement that speaks to both constituencies.

- Review your organization's core strategic documents with your brand goals in mind. See if they pass the brand test – read them as your customers would.
- Create a core brand message. Make it the one thing you want customers to experience as a result of dealing with your company.
- Define a few behavioral brand standards. Create guidelines from employees to bring the brand to life.

Jim Bolton,"Bringing Your Brand to Life," *Executive Excellence*, March 1999

Sadly for VW/Audi, the successful 5000 model was history. It was restyled and reintroduced under a new model numbering sequence to lukewarm reception. The brand had been tainted, and it took years for the taint to be removed. Only with the recent introduction of the new restyled A4, A6, and A8 series has Audi begun to recover. Brands that are tainted by a serious product problem take a long time to recover and some never recover completely.

Branding the culture

Building a company's culture into the brand's image

If you are assigned the job of tying together a branded product and a company's culture, where would you start? It may not be easy, but done well, it can be very powerful! A brand and a company are inseparable if the brand is a strong one and the company culture truly supports it. Saturn is the best example to illustrate how a company made a culture part of its brand. Only if all employees have a clear understanding of what the brand means and stands for can they embody it in everything they do. When that understanding is firmly embedded in the culture, it becomes a part of the brand. The Ritz-Carlton hotel chain developed this kind of brand reinforcement culture among its employees. Guests are not pointed to places they cannot find, they are taken there – and escorted by the Ritz-Carlton employee. Employees regularly ask if there is anything they can do to make the stay more pleasant. Service is uniformly good, and that culture of service is now a part of the Ritz-Carlton brand image.

Walt Disney attempted to ingrain this same kind of brand culture in its cast members when he was alive. His legacy lives on to this day. Notice that Disney does not call them employees. At Disney, everything is "the show" and the employees are "cast members". When they are at work, they are "on stage, and in costume" – even if that costume is nothing more than a clean, pressed blue oxford shirt and khaki slacks. Linking the brand to the culture of behavior has worked wonders for these companies and others like them. Southwest Airlines is another company where employees attempt to entertain and serve their guests, and have fun while they are doing it. The brand's image shows it!

KILLER QUESTIONS

Can you fix a damaged brand? What are the steps to take to decide whether it is worth fixing?

When the Culture can't manage the Brand

Levi Strauss & Co. have been one of the strongest global brands for many years. The Haas family managed the company and created a unique culture within Levi's. In the 1980s this unique culture saved the company in troubled times. Their approach to social values was heralded as proof that a company could be successful and have a conscience too.

Then, sometime in the early 1990s Levi's cultural values proved to be insufficient as source of a brand management know-how. In the decade of the 90s, Levi's share of the important age 14–19 males segment has dropped to half its earlier level. Ad campaigns have been ineffective, and new-product development stalled. Products were not on target with trends and consumers' lifestyles. Production costs and prices were too high. The company simply lost its way in spite of its culture.

Large customers were forced either to develop their own brands or add new, trendier brands to satisfy their customers. It wasn't that Levi's management didn't want to do the right things. It was that they didn't know the right things to do, to manage such a powerful and widely distributed brand of products. The family leaders were culture-conscious, but not trend-conscious merchants. The size and strength of the company insulated them for a time from the shocks of market share being undermined by GAP, Tommy Hilfiger, Lee, and others.

Changing a large, powerful and historically successful brand to match changing consumer tastes is a bit like turning a battleship around in a bathtub. It doesn't turn very quickly and there is precious little room for error. When a company manages with a collaborative culture to a great extent, the resultant meetings, task forces, teams, and memos lead to painfully slow decisions.

While all this was going on, new brands that Levi's executives barely knew about were taking its market share. Lee, GAP, and Calvin Klein were clearly on Levi's radar screen, but others like JNCO, Mudd, Fubu, Kikwear, Union Bay, Bongo, Stussy, Menace, Faded Glory, Arizona, and Canyon Blues became like an army of Lilliputians to Levi's Gulliver. Levi's' once dominant share evaporated to an army of fast-moving, trend-conscious, niche competitors.

Levi's couldn't believe that these outrageous styles were what their consumers wanted – that is, until sales continued dropping and plant closings loomed as the only solution to eliminate unneeded capacity and reduce operating costs. Further, Levi's became convinced that rapid delivery alone, even at premium costs, was worth the expense. Stores didn't care how fast the brand got there if it was with the wrong merchandise. Loyal consumers stopped going to the Levi's display first. The brand was crippled and is still trying to make a comeback.

Great brands die hard, and slowly, but once crippled; their recovery is often equally slow and painful. Late in its recovery process, Levi's adopted

The world's greatest brands have been the subject of numerous assessments of brand equity and brand value in the past. *Interbrand* has been at the forefront of developments in brand evaluation and has assessed the world's top brands ... The assessment is of *Brand Power*, the fullest possible view of each brand's strength and potential as a marketing and financial asset.

Brand Power is evaluated according to four dimensions:

- *brand weight* – the influence or dominance that the brand has over its category or market (more than just market share)
- *brand length* – the stretch or extension that the brand has achieved in the past or is likely to achieve in the future (especially outside its original category)
- *brand breadth* – the breadth of franchise that the brand has achieved both in terms of age spread, consumer types and international appeal
- *brand depth* – the degree of commitment that the brand has achieved among its customer base and beyond, the proximity, the intimacy and the loyalty felt for the brand.

Interbrand, *The World's Greatest Brands*

a Procter & Gamble style brand management structure, but results are still slow in coming. Indecision still marks its direction. Levi's is now also trying a multi-brand strategy, but competitors did this years ago. Only time will tell whether this legendary brand can recover – but it is unlikely that it will ever attain its prior brand and market share dominance.

A 25-step process of building & launching a brand

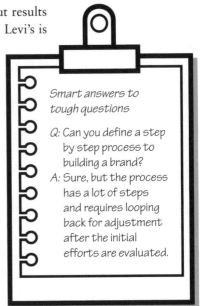

Plan

- Develop a strategy for the company, business unit, etc.

- Understand clearly what a brand is and is not, can do and cannot do.

- Research and understand the target market and audience for the brand.

- Determine the range of products and services to be branded, both initially and ultimately.

- Assign a brand manager/marketing manager to be responsible for the brand.

- Research and select a brand name(s), develop icons/logos and develop the brand strategy.

- Document the brand's origin and uniqueness and protect the brand with trademark and other intellectual property protection.

- Determine the brand's positioning vs. other brands and vs. competition.

- Develop a brand image/identity, character, personality, then document and communicate it broadly and clearly.

Develop

- Thoroughly research that image/identity, character and personality until it is completely understood, using focus groups, interviews, surveys, etc. as appropriate.

- Check to verify that the brand strategy matches the company strategy for these products, services, customers, markets, etc.

- Develop an implementation plan and the tactics that support the strategy for the product, service and brand.

- Prepare a brand launch plan, with accountabilities, budgets, timing, target markets, and expected results (and measures).

- Determine if test markets or other preliminary steps are necessary/desirable.

- Select an advertising agency (if necessary) or a public relations firm, etc.

Execute

- Design the brand's trade dress including product design/service design, packaging and presentation, merchandising (if applicable), etc.

- Develop advertising and promotion plans.

- Develop sales and distribution placement plans.

- Develop collateral materials to support the above plans.

- Set criteria for how, where and when to use the brand, its icon/logo(s), develop initial brand extension, sub-branding or co-branding guidelines.

- Sell the product/service into the desired distribution and produce the product or deliver the service.

Evaluate & adjust

- Measure the initial outcomes and opinions in terms of how purchasers and prospects who did not purchase perceived the brand vs. what was intended.

- Measure brand and advertising awareness, assess competitors' and customers' reactions.

- Based on initial outcomes and measures, make necessary adjustments to any/all of the above and return to the "Execute" section.

5

Brand Influence

HOW DO BRANDS INFLUENCE POTENTIAL PURCHASERS – BRAND AWARENESS, BRAND PREFERENCE AND BRAND LOYALTY?

There is a sequence that builds influence. First consumers must be aware of a brand, then develop a preference based on past favorable experience, word of mouth or the perception created by advertising and promotion and finally after repeated purchases, they may become loyal to the brand, and choose it over another competing brand.

Brand influence

Now that's loyalty!

Mark DiMassimo has his own New York agency, DiMassimo Brand

Advertising. Not too long ago, he surveyed 1500 people about their brand loyalty – and their marital fidelity. He had a hunch that there was a relationship between loyalty to a brand and loyalty to a spouse!

Sure enough, he found a connection, but it depended on the brand and whether it was a strong one or a weak one. A warning is in order. The scientific reliability of his study is not known, but the results are certainly interesting. Fully 70% of the people who preferred to bank with Chase Manhattan were unfaithful to their spouse. I wonder what kind of deposit and withdrawal plan that bank has for alimony checks. Pepsi drinkers admitted the next highest infidelity rate of the brands surveyed at 59%. Maybe this is a flaw of "the Pepsi Generation." People who bought GAP jeans were among the more loyal with only 19% straying from the path of marital fidelity, but fans of chocolate-maker Hershey were even more loyal at only 12% cheaters.

Since the news of the study did not divulge all of the brands surveyed, or the reliability of the methods used, conclusions are hard to reach. One

- *Customer loyalty* – the proportion of times a purchaser chooses the same product or service in a specific category compared to the total number of purchases made by the purchaser in that category, under the condition that other acceptable goods and services are conveniently available in that category. *Customer loyalty is a behavior. It is measured as a proportion.*
- *Customer satisfaction* – the attitude resulting from what customers think should happen (expectations) interacting with what customers think did happen (performance perceptions). *Customer satisfaction is an attitude and it is typically measured using some sort of attitudinal scale.*

William D. Neal (Sr. Exec. Officer, SDR, Inc.), "Satisfaction be Damned, Value Drives Loyalty," at ARF, Oct. 1998

thing is certain – brand loyalty is a powerful force, maybe more powerful than some spouses' marital loyalty. I think I'll put on my GAP jeans, and have a Coke (not a Pepsi) and a Hershey bar before I go to the bank (not Chase Manhattan). Perhaps my marriage will be safe if I am careful! Studies like this may be laughable, but brand awareness, preference and loyalty are no laughing matters to companies who spend millions of dollars building and promoting brand names.

Brand awareness

I will first use a story from my own personal experience to illustrate some of the important principles in this chapter, and then use examples to illustrate various aspects of brand awareness, preference, influence and loyalty.

When I started with Huffy Corporation in 1979, its bicycle business was split into two divisions, a large one in Ohio, and a smaller one in California. I was to start the third division, in Oklahoma. Its planned size was to fall in-between the other two, and the three division would split the US geographically and serve the areas where they were located.

Brand name was an important differentiator in Huffy's mass retail customer base of that era which consisted of Sears, Wards, Kmart, Wal*Mart (a very small retailer of $1 billion sales in 1979). There were a large number of outlets selling bikes, including many (now defunct) regional discount store chains such as TG&Y, Venture, W.T. Grant, Gibson, Gold Circle, and many others. Large auto stores like Western Auto and Pep Boys also sold bikes. National and regional hardware co-operatives like Ace, True Value, Coast-to-Coast, Servistar, etc., were active bike retailers, as were catalog showrooms like Service Merchandise and Best Products. Even some drug stores sold bikes! Many of these retailers sold bikes under their own private labels on the floor next to our Huffy branded bikes. Building our national brand was a challenge to say the least!

In the mid-1970s, Huffy had successfully introduced a new line of BMX bikes based on look-alikes of the popular moto-cross racing motorcycles. It was Huffy's first big hit advertised on TV and it launched the Huffy brand name into the big leagues, where Schwinn had dominated the US bicycle brand name market for several decades.

By the late 1970s and early 1980s Huffy had an "aided" brand awareness of just over 50%. At this point I should mention that there are three primary measures of brand awareness: Top of Mind, Unaided, and Aided awareness. The descriptions are shown in the box that follows. Huffy's goal was to catch and surpass Schwinn in all three.

In a few years, Huffy's combination of excellent distribution, consistent advertising and heavy retail promotion pulled us to the top of the heap. First we achieved our goal in aided awareness. When given a list of possible brand names to choose from, consumers virtually always recognized Huffy as a bike name. Next came the tougher challenge of unaided brand awareness. It was only after almost 15 years of advertising year-in and year-out that we began to catch the declining Schwinn brand name.

By 1991 Huffy Bicycles had achieved both the leading aided and unaided awareness among all consumers, and a top-of-mind awareness advantage over Schwinn with children and young adults – Huffy's primary advertising target market. Schwinn retained leadership among more mature adults, a result of their decades of US brand leadership, despite a near absence of advertising for the Schwinn name for several years. Its numerous Schwinn dealer stores around the country sustained the brand name.

Q: How is brand awareness measured anyway?

A: Brand awareness measures tell how strong a brand's presence is in the mind of consumers. There are three commonly used measures of brand awareness, and a fourth term that is useful to know:

- *Top-of-mind awareness* – the first brand recalled in a survey, with no prompting or mention/listing of possible brand names usually expressed as a percentage of the qualified respondents. Some respondents do not fit the demographic or geographic sample specifications, and their responses must not be counted or they will distort the results. This is sometimes referred to as *brand dominance*.
- *Unaided awareness* – one of the brands named in a survey of a given product or service class, with no prompting by mentioning of possible brand names, expressed as a percentage of qualified respondents. This is sometimes called *brand recall*.
- *Aided awareness* – recognition of a brand after being provided a list of names, which might be brands of the particular product or service, expressed as a percentage of qualified respondents. This is sometimes called *brand recognition*.
- *Brand salience* – the order in which brands come to mind; not what consumers think of the brand(s) but that they *do* think of them, and which ones they think of.

Many other ways of describing brand awareness exist, but nearly all of them are variations or combinations of these three.

Strong brands can even outlive company foolishness

There are two important lessons from this story. Strong brands, built over decades, often will out-live the market position of the company that built them. Brands can only be built progressively – first aided awareness must be built, then unaided awareness starts to grow, and finally, top-of mind awareness builds, but even more slowly. Consistent and persistent advertising and promotion are necessary to keep this progression moving.

Surveys of brand awareness information follow the sequence of "top of mind," "unaided" and "aided", to determine what percentage of the people surveyed are aware in differing degrees of the brands in a given product and market segment. As is the case of all surveys, it is important that the sample of people chosen (to call or interview) is properly selected, and is representative of the total market population for which the information is desired.

Sex sells brands – if done right

There is a term in the psychological science of persuasion called "likeable attractiveness." This describes the phenomenon of attributing more credibility or placing more trust in people who look like us or are very attractive. This is why models or good-looking people are used in ads or as product spokespersons.

In a recent ad campaign, Katrina Garrett, the female CEO of CrossWorlds computer software company, spent the company's entire ad budget on a single magazine ad. She is an attractive woman, so the ad pictured her in a

In an annual Monitor poll conducted by Yankelovich Partners, 74% of respondents "find a brand they like, then resist efforts to get them to change." Once consumers are convinced of the quality and value of a particular brand, it takes a lot of money and effort to change their minds.

Diane Crispell and Kathleen Brandenburg, *American Demographics* magazine, May 1993

simple, form fitting black dress with a deep V-cut neck. She was memorable – but until reminded recently, I could not even recall the name of her company! Did she advance her brand? Maybe, for the moment, but when the ad is memorable and the brand is not, it makes you wonder what was the point of advertising if not to create brand awareness and enhance the brand image.

Contrast this with the ad campaign of a few years ago, when English Leather cologne and after-shave lotions used a beautiful blonde model who simply said "My men wear English Leather … or nothing at all." Memorable? You bet! Attractive? Absolutely! But best of all, the brand is what was memorable. The ad worked.

On the other hand, graphic or sexual ads done in poor taste seldom do well. They turn off all but a very limited part of the audience. If that prurient minority is the target audience, the ad works for them, but that is a dicey proposition on which to build a brand.

Market research

Market research is an important step to gain the information needed to begin building a brand. There is more to doing research than simply asking some people a few questions. Some information can be gained that

Market research using surveys of customer satisfaction is no job for amateurs. Poor survey design can influence the results and conclusions – and all of the actions that follow could be based on flawed premises.

Surveys on intention to purchase or price that consumers will pay are only valid if the respondents vote with pictures of dead presidents or leaders of state (i.e., money!).

Smart things to say about brands

way, but basing major decisions on it is foolish. This is no place for amateur efforts. A professional design of the questions to be asked in market research is important because poorly designed questions can bias the results, leading the respondents to different answers from those they would otherwise give, as opposed to permitting a truly random and honest (unbiased) response. Using such biased answers as the basis for decisions can lead to very bad decisions!

Selecting a representative population to survey is a first step, then determining the sample size that will give the desired statistical reliability is next. The larger the sample, the better is the assurance that the sample of respondents is representative of the entire population, but the higher the cost of the research. Choosing how to qualify respondents as part of the target population is another crucial research issue. If possible, it is desirable to qualify them with as few questions as possible, thus devoting most of the survey time and cost to answering the questions that are the reason for the survey.

Written surveys are very sensitive to poor design, since there is no interaction between the interviewee and the interviewer. Poorly trained interviewers can also influence outcomes and cause inaccuracies. To emphasize the point again, this is not a field that should be left to amateurs. Too much can be riding on the outcomes of market research and brand research to do a sloppy job that leads to erroneous conclusions.

I raise these issues because there is a sequence of things you will need to know about a brand as it is being developed. The factors in this sequence are brand awareness, brand preference and brand loyalty, and all depend on surveys of one sort or another. Brand awareness information is almost entirely developed by surveying a representative population of prospective and current purchasers of the product or service in question.

Brand preference

Measuring brand preference

Brand preference is also traditionally determined by asking consumers which of several choices they would choose given various sets of circumstances. Brand preference survey information is informative but only directionally useful and far from absolute in its accuracy. Only when consumers "vote for their choices with money" – that is, make a purchase – do you really know which of the available brands they preferred on that day, in that situation. Market research about what people would hypothetically pay for something is notoriously inaccurate. Again the only way to know how much people would pay for something is to sell it to them. On the other hand, research as to which of several options a person would buy which are all in the same price range, is useful and can be directionally accurate.

Unfortunately, the real world is an imperfect place, and people may not choose the brand they prefer because of situational issues. The preferred brand may be out of stock, or not available in the size or color or package configuration desired. The competing brand may be on sale at a great price or be part of some other promotional offer. The competing brands may not all be merchandised in the same place, so all the choices are not readily available when a purchase is being made. Consumers may prefer a premium brand but may not be able to afford it. There may be another influencer involved in the decision (e.g. a spouse, a parent and a child).

Smart quotes

Don't get into arguments with idiots with biases, they'll drag you down to their level and then beat you with experience.

Thanks to columnist/humorist Dave Barry for this bit of wisdom

Merging companies doesn't necessarily merge brand preferences or loyalties

Wall Street appreciates the power and value of a brand name. Many companies advertise to impress investors as much as to influence consumers. I am not sure such a practice is a good idea, but where the financial community can be favorably influenced along with the targeted consumer, this is a win-win. When I was with Huffy Bicycles, we always made sure to advertise in the markets where the headquarters of our major customers were located as long as they were viable markets for our ad plans anyway. There is no harm in the buyer seeing the ad while he or she is relaxing at home before dinner.

Mergers and acquisitions can have a tremendous effect on brand awareness and brand character. When two companies are joined, such as the Daimler-Chrysler merger, what identity remains? Is the brand character the sum of, the average of, or totally different from the two individual companies. Years of accumulated preference can be trashed in a moment by a merger. I have always preferred BP gas stations just because of years accumulation of good, although small experiences. I never cared much for Amoco service stations because of a few bad experiences (or vice versa). Now BP and Amoco merge. The old Amoco station becomes a BP or vice-versa. What do I think?

The same kind of example could easily be used to describe banks, stockbrokers, accounting firms and many more situations. Unless the managers

> **Smart things to say about brands**
>
> When a merger makes it tempting to combine two brand names – don't do it. The usual result is to mess up the image of both brand names. Don't waste them competing with each other in the same market segments either. Carve out a separate niche for each brand.
>
> *Example: Daimler-Chrysler*

who handle the integration of the merged companies understand the respective brands' characters and images, they can inadvertently destroy what took years to build. Even if they do this kind of integration carefully, there are big risks – brand loyalty can be strong as steel or fragile as a thread.

Brand loyalty

Measuring brand loyalty is difficult

If brand awareness and brand preference are possible but challenging to measure via surveys, brand loyalty is even more complicated and more important to measure. One sure way to

KILLER QUESTIONS

How and how often will we measure brand awareness, brand preference and brand loyalty?

Q: Can you categorize typical brand influences by types of shoppers?
A: Yes. Here is one useful breakdown.

Type	% of total population*	Characteristic
Conformists	12%	want to belong to the crowd
Popularity seekers	12%	go for trendy brands
Sentimentals	12%	seek comfort & old-fashioned
Intellects	17%	upscale, technical, sophisticated
Relief seekers	17%	want escape from pressures
Actives	15%	like healthy, social lifestyle
Pragmatists	16%	just want their money's worth

*total 101% due to rounding error

Total Research Corporation (Princeton, NJ), *American Demographics*, May 1993

Smart answers to tough questions

measure brand loyalty is by recording repeat purchases of the same brand items in scanner based retail point-of-sale (POS) systems. Companies like Wal*Mart are building massive POS databases that are capable of yielding such data to its trading supplier-partners.

Other ways to check brand loyalty are via post-purchase surveys, often acquired via an on-line registration, a mail-in survey card included in the product, or via a personal follow-up (in the case of high-cost services or high-priced purchases like automobiles). Non-specific retail audits can also provide some brand loyalty data, but can be in error when they depend solely on the consumer's recall of the brand bought – and similar-sounding brands or highly popular brands often get confused.

While I was with Huffy Bicycles, the Huffy name became somewhat synonymous with mass-market bikes. Our major US competitor was Murray, and it was not unusual to receive post sale data that a consumer reported they bought a "Huffy Murray" bike. It was anybody's guess which brand they actually bought.

Brand loyalty is high where both status and perceived differences in results are combined

Titleist golf balls have a tremendous following among avid golfers. There is a difference among golf balls, but in blind tests, only the most discrimi-

As consumers streamline their lifestyles, branding becomes a dominating factor in consumer decision making ...7 out of 10 Americans agree ... 'I buy the same brand over and over again, without really thinking about it".

Kevin Clancy & Robert Shulman, *Marketing Myths that are Killing Business McGraw-Hill 1994*

nating professional golfers can demonstrably tell the difference. None-the-less, millions of weekend golfers still choose Titleist. More touring professionals use Titleist balls than any other and more tournaments are won by golfers using Titleist balls. Competitors would argue that this is due to Titleist paying more pro golfers endorsement fees to use their balls. It really doesn't matter as long as the mass of golf ball users have a brand image of Titleist as a superior ball that may or will help their golf game and lower their score.

Even if they admit the ball doesn't really help lower their score much or at all, there is the matter of "looking good." Many golfers spend huge amounts of money on expensive golf clubs of varying designs in hopes of gaining a slight performance advantage and a lower score. At least a part of these brand choices have to do with the brand's image and how it reflects on the user by adding status to them. It is far classier when asking a fellow golfer to help locate the ball on a stray shot to say "I am playing a black Titleist number 1" instead of some lesser cost, not-so-famous ball. Most golfers know that this is the kind of ball touring pros play with, and here is the weekend duffer, proudly playing the same golf ball – not just a close copy – exactly the same ball. Callaway Golf's Big Bertha brand clubs have developed a similar cachet. All of this kind of brand image-based loyalty is attributable to a small amount of performance enhancement and a large amount of brand image for status reasons.

Brand loyalty is very powerful

I am typing this on an Apple Powerbook. I have used Apple computers for 7 years, and in spite of their decline in market share, and fewer available

How brand loyalty can be segmented for strategic analysis:

- non-customers (who buy competing brands or do not use the product)
- price-switchers (who are very price-sensitive)
- passively loyal (who buy out of habit)
- fence-sitters (who are indifferent to choosing among several brands)
- committed (who will buy the brand consistently)

David A. Aaker, *Building Strong Brands* (The Free Press, 1996)

software titles, I continue to use them. I am brand-loyal. It is not because I like the Apple name *per se* – although I do. It is because Apple has built a following based on features and performance that are different from the numerous types of Windows-based PCs. To be honest, the latest versions of Windows are much more like Apple – but they are not the same in use or "feel"! The differences in look, feel, error messages, features, and so forth are the kinds of details that create the Apple brand's unique character and lead to fierce brand loyalty.

Steve Jobs understands this and is leading Apple back to a more meaningful position in the personal-computer market. Apple is playing to those brand character features in everything from the advertising theme "Think Different," to the striking styling and color variety of the new Apple iMac, G3 Mini-towers and G3 Powerbook laptops. Jobs understands what made Apple successful and is returning it to its roots. Even the omission of a floppy disk drive from the iMac was a statement of leadership in concept, even though Apple's 5% market share make it anything but a market leader in a broad sense of the word. Steve Jobs also knew the Apple faithful were hungry for leadership statements, no matter how small they are.

As long as he is at the helm (as interim CEO), Apple will sustain its brand-loyal followers. Apple's striking good looks, simplicity and ease of use, combined with its increasing compatibility with Internet browsers and Microsoft Windows programs (Word, Excel, and PowerPoint) will help it gain more loyal new followers.

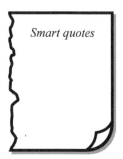

Smart quotes

Some considerations in brand loyalty:

- Value (price & quality)
- Image (both the brands' own personality and its reputation)
- Convenience and ease of availability
- Satisfaction
- Service
- Guarantee or warranty.

Ultimately, brand building involves giving the customer what she or he wants with value (price and quality) and the image the customer is seeking, aspiring to or at the very least ready and willing to accept. Building brand loyalty involves continuing to serve that customer in a satisfactory way.

The keys things to do:

- Know your customer
- Know what your customer wants
- Satisfy your customer
- Keep satisfying your customer
- Know when to stay the same and when to change
- Use your research.

Joe Marconi, *Beyond Branding* (Probus, 1993)

Customer retention is the bottom line of brand loyalty

Brand loyalty is an important and valuable outcome of creating brand awareness and preference. Ultimately brand loyalty means keeping the customer who previously bought the brand coming back and buying it again and again. An example of how one brand retains customers is Procter & Gamble's Tide detergent. The Tide brand name has existed for many years, and customers who know it, like it, and buy it year after year. Tide as a brand has undergone only minor changes in its apparent identity, or its orange and yellow sunburst box over the years. Yet, according to insiders, Tide's formulation has changed over 40 times! As fabrics change, laundry habits change, through the switch from hot to cold water for laundry, P&G. have revised the product so that it delivers on its brand promise – to get the clothes clean and white, without damaging colored items. An occasional "new, improved" showed up on the carton, but other than that, Tide has been an old reliable detergent brand, and by doing so, it has retained a loyal customer base for decades.

Intel has used the -86 and Pentium sub-brands in a similar fashion over recent years. "Intel Inside" became the umbrella brand. People who were satisfied with their 286 and 386 processor-based computers, were more likely to buy the 486 to satisfy their Intel Inside needs. Performance kept up with the times and needs (or at least perceived needs) of the computer user. When the -86 nomenclature had lived its useful life which was shorter

One of the most critical factors P&G has used to ensure that the brand loyalty is converted into customer retention is to ensure that the product continuously meets or exceeds the promise made by the brand. More simply stated, it has to perform well.

A retired P&G Marketing Executive

than Tide by far due to the rapid changes and short life cycles of computers, the Pentium sub brand was introduced Pentium is now going through its iterations of "new, improved" as Pentium II, MMX, Pentium III, etc.

Wisely, 3Com is attempting to do the same thing with its popular Personal Digital Assistant (PDA) the PalmPilot. First iterations carried the modifiers "personal" and "professional" and now it is on to the Palm III, Palm V and Palm VII – even skipping numbers at times to convey a jump in technology. Such approaches to capitalizing on brand loyalty are what create the bottom line – brand retention – and continued brand strength.

Peer influence can create brand loyalty

Teenagers are notoriously concerned about peer approval. This creates the brand marketers' ideal situation. Create a brand that is a "gotta-have" for teens and they will flock to it. Delia's Inc. sells funky clothes and accessories by direct marketing to girls between the ages of 10 and 24. Most of their sales go to pre-teens and teenagers. This market of teen girls is a huge one: 28 million consumers and $60 billion annual spending.

The popularity of the TV show, "Sabrina (the teenage witch)" fueled the popularity of teen-specific fashions. Teens were passing the information about Delia's from classified ads in their favorite magazines, *Cosmopolitan, Mademoiselle, Seventeen*, etc. An Internet site (www.gurl.com) and a boutique site (www.delias.com) for girls were followed by a boys site (www.droog.com); a home-furnishing store site for kids (www.contentsonline.com) also extended their merchandising reach.

Delia's Inc. racked up sales of $150 million only a few short years after the founder was begging for support from venture capitalists. The power of a unique brand in a niche that thrives on peer pressure, peer support and uses the networking power of today's cyber-community is a powerful brand

21st-century organizations have to compete on brands because they have nothing left. They can't get product differentiation; they can't get superior pricing, distribution or promotion; so branding strategy is it.

Don Schultz (President of Agora, Inc. and author of *Measuring Brand Communication Return on Investment*)

force indeed. More about this powerful combination of teens and the web is in the final chapter about the future of brands.

Brands based on true performance advantages can sell at premium prices

Titleist golf balls sell at premium prices based on their performance according to touring golf professionals. Gillette is another company which has made its brands the premier products in their categories by creating real and perceived performance advantages. Gillette's Sensor Excel and Mach III shavers, Oral B Cross-Action toothbrush, and Duracell "Copper-top" Ultra batteries are all brands which are positioned at the highest price levels and brand images in their respective categories. The products sell because they live up to the image and the promises of the brand name.

Maytag's Neptune washer is a breakthrough in design and actually does a superior job of stain removal, while using less water than competing brands. Colgate's Total toothpaste was proven in clinical tests to reduce plaque, and approved by the Food & Drug Administration, thus it occupies a similar performance advantage based brand position. Intel's Pentium processors have carved out a premium niche in computer chips in much the same way. As long as these companies' brands deliver on the performance promises and remain true to their brand character and image, the premium prices and profits will continue to come along.

A revealing study about market share and brand awareness

An eleven-year study of the US car-rental industry shattered some long-standing perceptions and built others in their place. Whether this single study is definitive will be argued by experts for years. I want to share it with readers here, along with a bit of a counterpoint following it – because there are some smart things to learn from it. The most important one is that *it is much harder to change a brand's image than it is to change the awareness of the brand.*

In the study, advertising impacts on the market share of the various companies showed clearly that 70% of the beneficial effect of advertising in the car-rental business was generated by increasing awareness – particularly unaided awareness. Advertising themes and slogans which were memorable were those that were repeated over many years, emphasizing the importance of continuity of the message. Themes that supported current brand image were far more effective than those that tried to create new imagery.

After all is said and done, advertising which drives home the brand salience and builds unaided brand awareness is the most powerful tool for building brand share. Changing the image of the brand is tough, but keeping the brand in the forefront of consumers' minds just takes money for intrusive advertising that clearly and frequently mentions the brand with consistency and regular repetition.

There is no such thing as awareness without an impression of image

Ed Holzer is a career advertising executive who is chairman of Lois EJL Advertising in Chicago. He is also a brilliant guy with strong opinions. The subhead of this section is his quote in response to the position taken from the study cited above! Ed continued, "how you build the brand is inextricably linked to the way your portray it in advertising." When I asked him about the concept of building awareness without trying to change the image of a brand, his reply was, "you can't do one without the other." As he went on, it became clearer to me that I agreed with him. "You can't build awareness of a brand (or a product, etc.) without providing information and creating impressions about the brand or product. Of course you can do it poorly and then you won't create much of an image you'd want for the brand, but still may create some (negative) awareness of the brand."

Ed proceeded to tell me a true story from earlier in his career, when his firm was working for PaperMate pens. PaperMate made good, low-cost pens, but realized that it would be tough to move that brand-name upscale to compete with A.T. Cross, so they were looking for a more prestigious brand-name to buy, license, etc. They talked with many companies to no avail, but one such meeting had a profound effect on Ed's viewpoint about brand image. It was a meeting with Bulgari, the prestigious jewelry store name.

There was a presentation of their writing-instrument product line. The pens were brought out on polished brass trays draped with velvet, and shown one at a time. They were exquisitely made with gold, silver, jewels, and engraving. Each one was more beautiful and expensive that the previous one. $2000, $2500, $3000 and up were the prices. The impression of this brand was so clear and so dramatically upscale that there was no doubt it was the pinnacle of prestige in a writing instrument – until someone took one apart. As they unscrewed the jeweled, engraved gold barrel, out fell … a PaperMate refill!

The presentation of this brand created the overwhelming belief and left no doubt that these pens are anything but very expensive and prestigious. This experience and a lifetime in the business of building and advertising branded products and services led to the words Ed Holzer said to me on this day, "presentation is everything! The psychologists call it 'the set and setting' that work hand in hand. The set creates the mindset, the setting brings the experience to bear on the mindset."

In Holzer's succinct and confident definition, "Advertising is nothing but presentation. Whether you do it well or poorly creates an impression about a brand. The only variable is how well you do it and what impression results – not an either/or question of your building awareness or changing the image. You do both at once …"

Branding a country?

Before we leave this chapter, let's imagine things that are not normally considered in discussions about brands and branding. How about entire countries? Who said you cannot brand a country? Not David Lightle. He was faced with the amazing task of creating a brand for a country – Taiwan. We all know of brands that are identified with specific countries, and somewhat define our image of what those countries stand for in their products. For example:

- Germany: Mercedes-Benz, BMW – mechanical technical excellence

- Japan: Sony, Panasonic – electronic sophistication

- France: Chanel, Louis Vuitton – style and fashion

- Switzerland: Rolex, Swatch – precision timekeeping

- USA: Coke, McDonald's – the good leisure lifestyle, *or*
  Intel, Microsoft, IBM – leadership in information technology.

The Taiwanese who escaped from mainland China during Mao Tse Tung's era with little but a mountainous island and their fiercely proud heritage, continue to fear being absorbed by the People's Republic of China. Taiwan also feared that their rapid industrial growth and technological expertise were vastly under-appreciated by the broad majority of Americans. Only business people who had traveled there and seen their capabilities could appreciate how far this small island country had come in the last 2–3 decades as a world innovation and manufacturing power.

Around 1988, a group of four leading Taiwanese manufacturers decided to form the Brand International Promotion Association (BIPA). These four were top-quality, world-competitive companies: Acer (computers), Giant (bicycles), Proton (consumer electronics) and ProKennex (sporting goods, especially tennis racquets). They knew that there were other Taiwanese companies that would enjoy the benefits of branding if only they could mobilize them into supporting such an initiative. David Lightle's task, quite simply stated, was to elevate the image of Taiwan as a brand name for a country of origin of quality products, which provided innovation and value!

Lightle tells the story with a zeal that can only come from having lived it. From his roots in political positions in Taiwan, to supporting the startup

SMART VOICES

of world-renowned Saatchi & Saatchi's Taiwan advertising, David Lightle was very much the internationalist. He describes the path developing countries take as they evolve. Starting with light industry and agriculture to meet their own needs, they then begin to export, usually as an OEM (Original Equipment Manufacturer) supplying low cost products. As the country's competence grows, it moves up the ladder to more capital-intensive or service-intensive businesses aiming for higher product specifications and prices. This ultimately leads them to making their own products and needing some kind of brand name to assign the higher value to.

At some point during this evolution, most of these countries go through the counterfeiting stage. Their competence has grown sufficiently that they can make credible and functionally acceptable counterfeits of major branded products. Even the US went through this era in the post-revolutionary war period where many counterfeits of English products were made in the US. In this century, Japan, Taiwan and Korea have all moved through this stage, and progressed to making legitimate branded products of their own.

As China moved aggressively into manufacture of products previously made in Taiwan, the Taiwanese knew they must move upscale or lose their industrial base. The first phase of the Taiwan branding effort focused on quality, in an attempt to change the low-quality image brought about by Taiwan's developmental years. While Lightle argued against such a blatant assault on an area of perceived weakness, the campaign went forward. A theme, "It's very well made in Taiwan" was coined and promoted extensively with only moderate success. Target markets were the leaders of the developed world: US, Canada, Western Europe, Japan, Australia/New Zealand, etc. The awareness of Taiwanese products was aided, but the question remained as to whether many attitudes about them were changed. Was the brand image really being altered by such ads? Remember earlier sections about how difficult it is to change images that are deeply ingrained.

By 1993, after almost five years of the campaign, several Gallup surveys were held to assess the effectiveness of the campaign and determine the next direction. Research indicated that to build on Taiwan's strength, two areas were worthy of emphasis: Value and Innovation. These were areas in which Taiwanese products were recognized. As is often the case, the name chosen to portray these attributes of the "brand" Taiwan came about almost accidentally. During a casual after-hours discussion, Lightle told a colleague "I don't want to advertise two different positions. It will confuse the audience and fragment the campaign. I wish I could just have one word that covers both – like Innovalue!" "That's it," the colleague said! "Taiwan, your source for Innovalue."

The theme was chosen and the campaign is now in the final year of its 10-year plan, and a new, revised plan is being developed. Whether Taiwan as a brand has grown directly as a result of this campaign, the stature of Taiwan as an industrial power has certainly flourished. David Lightle points out that, "while brands may seem insignificant in the scheme of world politics and culture, they are not. A series of product or brand images favorable for a country can help overcome cultural deficiencies and even cultural atrocities. Most of all, in an era of serious global over-capacity in export markets; deflation can quickly sweep the globe. The rush to differentiate itself in a global market can be of critical importance to a country.

Just as brands can outlive companies, they can also outlive governments and mistakes – if they are properly launched, built and supported. At this very moment, several Latin American countries are working on similar initiatives – such as Colombia, wishing to shed its image as the home of drug lords, and build one as a major world supplier of a variety of products, including some of the finest coffees.

Clearly brands are far more important than it appears at first glance!

6

Brand Extensions

WHAT ARE LINE EXTENSIONS OR SUB-BRANDS AND HOW CAN BRANDS BE OVEREXTENDED OR ABUSED?

When a strong brand is extended in use to apply to products that are too different, or used in conjunction with another different brand, consumers can become confused or suspicious. Excessive dilution of a brand, especially on products that do not fit with the brand's name, image or character, can damage brands. So can failing to live up to the promise made by advertising or promotion.

Brand extensions

One of the simplest things to do is to extend an existing, well-known brand to additional products or services. It is also one of the most dangerous things to do. The temptation to do a branded line extension is so great because, when it works, it transfers the valuable secondary meaning of the brand to the new offering. Examples of successful brand extensions are obvious when they work, as in the case of Diet Coke.

Brand extensions, simple and effective or simply dangerous – the debate continues

Failures in brand extensions are not always so obvious, because the damage they do to the primary brand may take time to show. Often such damage is subtle, as the case with 7Up. The total sales of 7Up branded products barely increased at all, but the brand was fragmented among 3 or more extensions raising costs and diluting the primary brand's impact.

A great example of this kind of brand extension subtlety is the comparison of Colgate-Palmolive and Procter & Gamble done by Al Ries and Jack Trout in their classic 1981 marketing book *Positioning: The Battle for your Mind* (McGraw-Hill 1981 & Warner Books 1986). They cite the many brand-extension house-names of Colgate-Palmolive: Colgate toothpaste, Colgate toothbrushes, Palmolive dishwashing liquid, Palmolive hand soap, etc. P&G, however, use unique brands, each of which has a distinctive image: Tide makes clothes white, Cheer makes then "whiter than white," while Bold makes them "bright". This is much clearer imagery for consumers – each brand means something unique. With fewer brands, P&G did twice as much volume and made five times as much profit.

Too many varieties of a good brand get beaten by specialists – or do they?

If this kind of conclusion is not convincing enough, Jack Trout supported his prior viewpoint in his 1996 update book *The New Positioning* (McGraw-Hill 1996). Two examples of line-extension brand strategy were Scott, the leading brand of toilet tissue whose name was extended into

> Trying to extend a seemingly all-powerful brand to increase volume can end in despair if you aren't successful. It will taint your image in existing markets and damage your brand name.
>
> Guy Kawasaki (author of *Rules for Revolutionaries*), cited in "Old habits that can kill new products", *Fortune* magazine, 24 May 1999, p. 296

Scotties, Scottkins, Scottowels, etc. Soon the brand becomes so non-specific it no longer conveys a useful shorthand value picture. In a relatively few years after this over-extension, P&G's Charmin brand overtook Scott to become the number-one toilet tissue.

But even Procter & Gamble aren't impervious to this temptation of brand extension. P&G had the leader in solid shortenings, Crisco, when the world began moving to cooking oil. They decided to extend the brand and make Crisco Oil. What became the best selling oil? Wesson Oil! When corn oil comes into fashion, Wesson succumbs to making Wesson Corn Oil. The brand leader then becomes Mazola Corn Oil. As margarine begins to use corn oil, of course Mazola introduces Mazola Corn Oil margarine, which, of course, is beaten at the supermarket by brand specialist Fleischmann's. The message is simple – brand specialists beat brand extensions more often than not!

The opponents of this view would cite Coke's dominance of the soft-drink aisle with Coke, Diet Coke, Caffeine Free Coke, Caffeine Free Diet Coke, and Cherry Coke against specialists like RC's Diet Rite or Dr. Pepper. There is little doubt that distribution strength has something to do with the success of brand extensions. So, also, does the underlying strength of the brand being extended and the similarity of products where the extension is being used.

People who prefer soft drinks like Coke almost as much for its familiar reliability and omni-presence as for its specific taste. If they liked the taste so much why did the "better tasting" New Coke fail so miserably? Brand preference is a complex combination of familiarity, habit, quality, service (easy, convenient availability in this case), cost (Coke is often promoted at very low prices) advertising (after all it is "The Real Thing!"), and much more.

For years, the US two major candy companies, Mars and Hershey's had different philosophies about their brand names. Mars had unique names: M&Ms, Snickers, Milky Way, Almond Joy, Three Musketeers, etc. For many years, Hershey's candies were almost all Hershey's and only occasionally followed by sub-brands like Krackel, Mr. Goodbar, etc. Only in more recent years Hershey's began using unique brands more of the time.

This leads us to the conclusion that blindly endorsing or categorically condemning brand extensions are probably both wrong. A wise old sage once told me, "always avoid saying always and never say never". Maybe this is a good rule to remember. Like "Value," the brand's ability to be extended is situational. Too much extension is likely a bad idea, since it provides more opportunities to blur what the consumer associates with the brand. Too little may be under-utilizing a valued asset. Finding the right place to stop is tough!

> **Smart things to say about brands**
>
> Always avoid always and never say never.
>
> This leads us to the conclusion that either blindly endorsing or categorically condemning brand extensions are probably both wrong. The right answer depends on the circumstances and objectives for the brand.

Cannibalization is a by-product of line extensions

One of the most challenging decisions encountered in line-extension strategy is how to regard cannibalization. Cannibalization occurs when extended brands eat into the sales of the parent brand. Consider Cheerios cereal. General Mills has now produced Honey Nut Cheerios, Apple Cinnamon Cheerios, Frosted Cheerios, Multi-Grain Cheerios and Team Cheerios. In their zeal to leverage the highly regarded Cheerios brand, they had modified it with a whole armada of extensions – but have they sold more total Cheerios? Perhaps they have, but what effect has this long list of brand extensions had on sales of the original Cheerios? Almost certainly those sales have declined as a result of self-cannibalization. One strategist would say that it is better for them to cannibalize their brand rather than a competitor to do so. But what if no competitor was threatening them by successfully selling round, toasted oat cereal. Then whom did they cannibalize and how profitably?

KILLER QUESTIONS

If our brand is strong, how can we or should we extend it to other products or services, and with what limitations?

Obviously, the desire to have a sweeter version of Cheerios drove their initial efforts which, like Tide – were geared to customer retention in the face of changing tastes. The real issue is how much extension is too much. The answer unfortunately is usually found only after reaching and exceeding that point! In their positioning book, Ries and Trout described a similar phenomenon previously mentioned, involving 7Up. It was the Un-cola, and that was very successful. Then the Un-cola became four or five varieties – Diet, Cherry, diet-cherry, etc. Sales of Un-cola never rose in proportion to the variety and the costs added by that variety – and I would bet the same is true with Cheerios! The result – incrementally more sales, less profit and potentially a confused and fragmented brand image with loyal customers.

Brand proliferation to excess is almost always bad

You can get a headache trying to cure a headache! Go to any drug store and brand-extension proliferation of the headache- and cold-medicines will give you headaches. Johnson & Johnson, the parent of Tylenol, the clear brand winner in acetaminophen-based (non-aspirin) pain relievers decided to go hog wild with extensions. Now there is Sinus Tylenol, Tylenol Cold medicine, Tylenol Cold & Flu, Tylenol Cold & Flu Severe Congestion formula, with and without cough suppressants, non-drowsy (notice no one advertised a "drowsy" formula – just the non-drowsy). The shelf is full of bottles that say Tylenol, but they lose to specialists over and over where the specialists stay focused. Fortunately for Tylenol, several of their competitors followed the same flawed brand logic, which effectively leveled the competitive playing field and gave them a chance to do OK.

The halo effect can help another brand

While brand extensions are easy but dangerous, often strong brands can lend a halo effect to give a new, similar brand a lift. Snickers benefited by a tag line "from the makers of Milky Way." Milky Way's established consumer awareness and loyalty was strong enough that simply tying the two brands together validated the new product as one to buy and try.

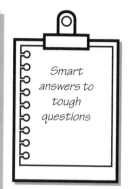

Smart answers to tough questions

Chaps by Ralph Lauren created an upscale image for a mid-scale, department-store brand. Alone, Chaps would have been an acceptable brand name, but when it was associated with the Ralph Lauren prestige "halo" it became an excellent brand. On the other hand, the children's clothing by Osh Kosh b'Gosh benefited from the durability of the older "overall maker's" brand name, but suffered from not having a youthful image. Halos can only extend so far.

Entertainment brands, particularly TV shows, use this halo effect flagrantly. Spin-offs of popular TV shows are a common way to launch new shows on the coat-tails of successful older brands (shows). The new comedy subtitled "by the makers of Seinfeld" brings the viewer in at least once. Then the product has to earn its own brand preference. The halo must relate the two products in similar categories so the consumer gives some credit for transfer of some expertise. "From the producers of ER," will get a new drama a better audience than saying, "from the producers of America's Funniest Videos."

If the product included in the halo doesn't measure up to the expectations created, the halo of the original product can be tarnished. What if Snickers tasted awful? Perhaps people would conclude that the makers of Milky Way were not so hot themselves, and Milky Way sales might drop. If the new TV show from the makers of Seinfeld is dud, viewers will be skeptical if that halo is ever used again. Like brand extensions, halos cut both ways, and must be used with caution.

KILLER QUESTIONS

Are we willing to or can we benefit from co-branding with other brands and how?

Co-branding for best effect

If you study the market for a few moments, you will find an increasing number of places where co-branding is being used to promote the image of two well-known brands in a single offering. You have probably deduced that where the brand fit is good, this works very well. The most notable ones are in the food industry, but there are many others.

Ice cream and frozen yogurt stores all offer toppings and mixture ingredients for the various concoctions. Nabisco's Oreo brand cookies, M&Ms candies, Snickers, Heath, and Butterfinger candy bar chunks are among examples where a proven known brand is mixed with another product to the benefit of both brands. A smart brand builder realized that the well known brand additions adds credence to the ice cream or yogurt brand much the way Heinz ketchup was being perceived as a positive enhancement in a restaurant by my wife.

Kellogg's Pop Tarts are a popular supermarket brand of breakfast and lunch pastry. These are made more attractive when their fruit flavors are provided by Smucker's, a premium producer of jellies and jams. Ford's Bronco sport utility vehicle and outfitter/clothier Eddie Bauer co-branded on a vehicle successfully. In computers, the "Intel inside" logo, even on a

Hewlett Packard computer, is a commonly seen co-brand that signals a "premium" processor chip – and usually a premium price too! Always remember that brands are all about sending messages to potential purchasers.

In other cases, such co-branding makes little sense if the product families and brands involved are not a particularly good fit. Levi's has added its brand to many items that are a stretch for the consumer to see how the Levi's jeans brand adds much value – backpacks, school portfolios, even shoes are only mediocre fits with the Levi's brand image.

On the other hand, a few brands have such a loyal, niche following, they add their special type of co-branding value to almost anything. Harley-Davidson motorcycles is one of these brands. Whether it is on jackets, t-shirts, or even tattoos – Harley followers love that brand. When was the last time you heard of a brand name so strongly identified with its customers that they chose to have it permanently tattooed on their body? Harley-Davidson has that kind of brand strength. While Nike's powerful brand is reaching far from its initial shoe product core brand, it is staying within the sporting industry as a brand focus.

What new brand extensions might come next?

The Internet and lifestyles provide ample opportunities for brand extensions. Bookseller amazon.com is branching out into music CDs, auctions, drugstores and far, far beyond. Will the brand carry broad extensions?

> Make sure halos, co-brands or brand extensions don't undermine the primary brand by failure to deliver on the promises made. When this kind of failure happens, the primary brand can be damaged! What looks like a "no-brainer", turns into one – but the wrong way.

Smart things to say about brands

Since all are based on purchases via their Internet web sites, this new kind of extension has an unusually broad reach. History says they will go too far and get beaten by specialists.

Starbucks is filling every nook and cranny with coffee bars, shops, and kiosks. What comes next? Starbucks food of course! Since it already sell the kinds of food that go well with coffee, it will assume it can successfully sell other kinds. The odds are that it can't – at least not profitably. Its model is based on a simple modular menu of high margin, coffee related products with minimal spoilage. Restaurant style offerings will not fit that model, nor will it fit the brand image. Starbucks is coffee – but it may not be "food" in general. We'll see!

KILLER QUESTIONS

Should we use sub-brands along with our primary brand, and how?

Other airline carriers will feel compelled to mimic Southwest Airlines' efficient, fun and very profitable short-haul airline. As it lengthens its routes, Southwest takes a risk. Remember the failed People's Express. It forgot what it was that made it successful and tried to be everything to everybody. Southwest's risk is not nearly as great as United, Delta, or American if they attempt to be both a brand for a full service airline *and* a brand for a no-frills short-hop airline. Brand image conflicts like that make consumers confused, and when consumers are confused, they stop buying, and both brands suffer.

The bottom-line – "to extend or not to extend" –
that is the question!

The answer to this much debated issue is yes, and no. In creating unique brands like P&G does, it is advisable when and if there are the resources available to properly launch and support the unique brand, and market potential to justify that level of spending on a single brand. Another ca-

Extensions can bring diminished returns if lowest common denominator perceptions are passed on to the parent brand. P&G learned this lesson painfully when they attempted to extend Ajax, their strong abrasive cleanser line to other products, to compete with Comet and others. Not only did the extension not succeed, but consumers, disappointed with the less than stellar performance of some Ajax line extensions, transferred the "lowest common denominator" of performance to the parent brand, damaging it.

On the other hand, Ivory bar soap's fame for gentleness was fairly successful when extended to dishwashing liquid where gentleness on the hands is a major benefit. This worked because the formulation of dishwashing liquid was gentle. In fact, according to P&G insiders who prefer not to be quoted, Tide detergent has changed formulation literally hundreds of times over the years. In this case it was necessary to maintain performance in the face of changing laundry conditions, equipment, fabrics, water temperatures, etc. Sometime the best way to extend a brand is to extend its performance but not its name.

A former P&G Marketing executive

veat is that the single brand's name must be carefully and skillfully chosen to convey the right differentiated image to prospective consumers.

When there is a well known brand with a strong reputation, extending that brand to other products is fine, unless it becomes so diluted that it weakens the meaning on all of the products. Umbrella brands can transfer an image of dependability, but they must be accompanied with sub-brands or product names that finish the communication process. Titleist makes several kind of golf balls, each with a selected set of characteristics and a name that is indicative of those characteristics. They have been less successful selling clubs, since consumers think of Titleist as a golf ball brand! Strength like this can be a treasure for the core product but a detriment to extending the brand.

Cobra, another subsidiary of Fortune Brands (Titleist's parent company) is golf-club brand, and will likely fare less well using the brand on golf balls. If anyone doubts this, simply consider how long Callaway, the leading golf-club maker has been pondering, developing and waiting to launch its golf ball line – it was 2½ years as of this writing. Only Microsoft can take longer to promise something's coming and not trigger uproarious laughter!

LAUNCHING AN UMBRELLA BRAND FOR SUB-BRAND EXTENSIONS

Steve Goubeaux is one of the partner-owners of Visual Marketing Associates (VMA) which is a marketing and design firm (graphic & industrial) located in the historic Livery building in Dayton OH. The firm was founded by Steve's partner, Ken Botts after a successful career in the Huffy Bicycle Design Center. Steve was top sales and marketing executive for a couple of major consumer products businesses prior to joining Ken at VMA. Together they have formed one of those symbiotic relationships that builds a unique company and several major brands for clients.

CharBroil, the US leading barbecue grill maker is one of VMA's clients. So is Suncast, a market leader in garden hose-reels and home/garden storage products. VMA also helped launch the product lines and create the brand name for InGear Sports with yet another Huffy Bike "alumnus", Kevin Achatz, (one of InGear's founders). InGear was named one of Entrepreneur magazine's fastest-growing small companies – formed without the help of venture capital. Steve explains InGear's brand strategy, which he termed "An umbrella brand strategy with 'product family line-extensions.' The concept was to create a well-known trade brand name as the brand umbrella, and then use 'product-family consumer brands' for specific product lines." This approach is inversely related to line extensions – in this case the extension was planned up-front, as part of the initial branding strategy.

Steve relates why the "InGear" umbrella brand was chosen "The brand had to be a widely applicable, non-limiting umbrella name yet one that was memorable, sporty, aggressive, forward-moving and could support strong series of product families. The company knew it couldn't spend enough advertising money to launch the brand name with consumers, so it targeted major mass-retailers and made shelf space for the trade brand name and its contextual variations their objective." The sub brand name for line extensions would then be descriptive enough to cue the consumer about what kind of product family it stood for.

Under the InGear umbrella they then positioned product family brands for different product categories: FROZ'N for cooler products, Expedition for backpacks, OCEANA for water sports products and so forth. The umbrella brand was always on the products but in a supporting role – on zipper pulls, on small Levi's style tabs, and in statements like "by InGear" following the product line's specific brand. The result is a trade brand that has become well known to retail buyers, and gained the shelf space necessary to meet its sales objectives. Individual product family brands are just now becoming familiar to consumers after several years of repeat store shelf appearances and retailer ad promotions, In this case line extension was planned before the fact and became part of a core brand strategy.

Steve and VMA continue to work very closely with his Kevin and his partners at InGear. Because, as Steve puts it, "We can talk to them honestly and help them with one of the biggest challenges of this guerilla marketing style of brand development – that is maintaining consistency and continuity of the brands and not applying them if they don't fit."

Line extensions that are planned up front, under the umbrella of a strong trade brand can be a good way to leverage recognition without big budgets.

Umbrella brands offer the potential for competitors who could never compete head-to-head with the P&Gs of the world on a brand by brand basis to spread their brand reputation equity over a stable of products with considerably less ad spending per product. But it is critical that all of the products in the family live up to the promises made – or else all will suffer.

7

Protecting a Brand

CAN YOU LOSE A BRAND NAME IF IT IS IMPROPERLY USED?

The laws on copyrights, trademarks and other intellectual property considerations are valuable to protect brands, but vary around the world. Becoming too much of a household word can be dangerous to a brand's trademark. If you plan to invest heavily in building a brand, make careful plans to protect it from infringement by competitors.

Protecting a Brand

Too strong can mean "too bad!"

If a brand name becomes so successful and dominant that it is the only name consumers remember for a given product, a dangerous thing can

happen. The name becomes accepted as a part of the language and the trademark protection for it can be lost. Famous names that have lost their trademarks are names like Nylon, Aspirin, Cellophane and Escalator. Others that came dangerously close are Jell-O, Kleenex, Scotch, Xerox, and Formica.

If this section comes out sounding kind of legal that is because many of the common forms of protection for brands and brand names are based on laws. You need to know about these laws; how they do and don't protect brands from being copied or stolen; and the technical interpretation of the

Smart quotes

Don't try knockoff names. If you call your on-line retailer buy-com.com, the real buy.com may come after you. What does it take, besides originality to win a trademark? A name that is more than merely descriptive. Cold Roast Beef, for example, probably wouldn't make it as a lunch meat brand, unless the owner could prove that customers associate that name with his product. HoneyBaked Ham did just that, registering its name after decades of brand-building. The strongest names – and those easiest to protect – spring from the imagination. Some of the most memorable are indistinguishable from their products: Kodak, Kleenex, Kool-Aid. Try coming up with a name that suggests what your business does without describing it. That means ditching obvious words like "medi" if you provide a health care product or service, or "gen" if you're involved in biotech.

Leigh Gallagher, *Forbes*, 19 April 1999.

legal word *infringement*. These laws may vary somewhat from country to country, but most countries have something similar to the US laws, and many countries cooperate with each other on enforcement of intellectual property laws.

The more common problem is infringement of the intellectual property rights of brands by creating very similar sounding or looking names or icons in order to trade on the brand equity of a well known brand.

KILLER QUESTIONS

What kind of protection can we get for our brand – trademarks, copyrights, etc.?

Trademarks – the first line of protection

The first kind of intellectual property protection that is a Smart Thing to Know About is trademark protection. Trademarks and

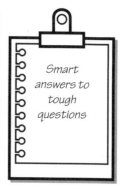

Smart answers to tough questions

Q: Is there such a thing as too much brand-name usage?

A: There is a serious risk if a brand name moves from being a brand identification to a generic part of the language to describe that type of class of product or service. Three well known names lost their trademark protection because they became generic terms for the product:

Aspirin pain reliever, Cellophane plastic sheet film, and Escalator people movers were all once brand names for companies that made those products.

This is why 3M calls it Scotch Brand tape, Kimberly Clark calls it Kleenex Brand tissue, and so forth. Adding the word "brand" is intended to keep the name from becoming generic and resulting in the loss of the trademark protection. Formica Brand laminated counter tops and Xerox Brand copiers are also trademark brands that flirted with disaster.

Federal Express could have been in similar jeopardy. We all speak of Xeroxing things and FedExing packages, but that makes those companies happy and sad at the same time – especially if you are Xeroxing on a Canon copier or FedExing using UPS Next Day.

Service Marks are words, names, symbols, or icons used by creators and sellers of goods and services to identify them and to distinguish them from those made and sold by others. For example, the Apple logo with its distinctive shape and the one with multi-colored bands are trademarks of Apple Computer.

For trademarks used in the US, federal trademark protection is available under the Lanham Act. Many states have trademark-registration statutes that resemble the Lanham Act, and all states protect unregistered trademarks under the common law of trademarks.

Trademark protection is available for words, names, symbols, or icons that distinguish the owner's goods or services from those of others. A trademark that merely describes a class or type of goods, rather than being a distinguishing symbol of the trademark owner's goods from those provided by others, cannot be protected. For example, the term "PC" cannot be protected as a trademark for computers because that term describes a type of computer that is sold by a number of manufacturers rather than distinguishing one computer manufacturer's goods.

KILLER QUESTIONS

Can you lose a brand name if it is improperly used?

A trademark that very closely resembles one already in use (in a given country) and that would be likely to cause confusion or mistake cannot be protected by a registration. In addition, trademarks that are "descriptive" of the functions, or nature of the products or services have special requirements they must meet before they can be protected.

The best trademark protection is received via filing a trademark registration application with the US Patent and Trademark Office. This can cost as little as $250 if you do it yourself and more like $2000 if you use a law firm to handle it for you. The Patent and Trademark Office is usually very busy, so backlogs and waits of several months are not uncommon.

You can try to protect yourself in the meanwhile by doing your own search of existing applications awaiting federal approval at the web site: www.uspto.gov. This won't be a complete search because there are always pending applications that take up to a couple of months to make it onto this list. To make a more complete search requires actually going to the agency's headquarters in Arlington, VA and physically make the search there.

Federal law also protects unregistered trademarks, but such protection is limited to the geographic area in which the trademark is actually being used. There is also a state trademark protection under common law which is obtained simply by adopting a trademark and using it in connection with goods or services. This protection is also limited to a geographic area in which the mark is actually being used. State statutory protection is obtained by filing an application with the appropriate state trademark office, but is limited in scope and not nearly as good as a federal trademark. State trademarks are sometimes valuable to retail establishments who have no desire to open branches outside their local area.

One overlooked aspect of trademarking a name is that the date of usage and sale in interstate commerce (in the US) often determines who has the earlier rights to a name in a conflict. A smart thing to do to protect a trademark is to make a usable sample of the product bearing the brand name and sell it for a reasonable price, but it must be sold in interstate commerce (between locations in different states in the US) to an independent party, not one of your employees! This action provides time (at least a year) to get the product into normal production without waiting for normal production to protect the brand name.

Trademark laws protect the owner's commercial identity (goodwill, reputation, and investment in advertising) by giving the trademark owner exclusive rights to use the trademark on the type of goods or services for which the owner has been or is using the trademark. Trademark owners can obtain injunctions against the confusing use of their trademarks by infringers, and they can collect damages for infringement.

There is one other catch you should know about. You can file for a trademark application, win approval and still get in trouble. Thanks to common-law rights, during the first five years of registration a company that can prove that it's been using the name can challenge your registration! You may be able to win this kind of challenge, but it still represents a risk – especially if you have not been using the name much or at all and the other company has used it widely.

Copyright Law – know what it is... and is not

There are two reasons why it is important to be familiar with the basic principles of copyright law. Copyright law is a "federal" law and the law does not vary from state to state (although the interpretation of the law may be different in different courts). This book is protected by copyright law, but your brand may not be.

While brands are not very well protected by copyright protection, this is sometimes part of a "web" of total protection that may include several of the legal forms of protection – trademarks, design patents, copyrights, etc. The listing that follows identifies the kinds of work that might be protected by copyrights. There are several items (underscored) that could be a

Smart answers to tough questions

product or part of a product. These could include the package containing and depicting the product or ads with an advertising tag line that becomes an integral part of the brand itself.

Copyright protection is available for "works of authorship," which include the following types of works:

- *Literary works* – novels, nonfiction prose, poetry, newspaper articles and newspapers, magazine articles and magazines, computer software, software manuals, training manuals, manuals, catalogs, brochures, ads (text), and compilations such as business directories

- *Musical works* – songs, advertising jingles, and instrumentals

- *Dramatic works* – plays, operas, and skits, pantomimes and choreographic works, ballets, modern dance, jazz dance, and mime works

- *Pictorial, graphic, and sculptural works* – photographs, posters, maps, paintings, drawings, graphic art, display ads, cartoon strips and cartoon characters, stuffed animals, statues, paintings, and works of fine art

- *Motion pictures and other audiovisual works* – movies, documentaries, travelogues, training films and videos, television shows, television ads, and interactive multimedia works

- *Sound recordings* – music, sounds, or words.

Copyright protection occurs automatically when an "original" work of authorship is created in a tangible form. In English, this means when you write something and "publish it" the copyrights are yours – automatically. Registration with the Copyright Office can be filed, but is usually not

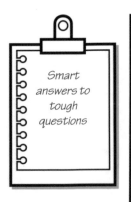

Smart
answers to
tough
questions

Q: Are there some places to find more information on this kind of protection?
A: There are many of them – here are a few for the US:

The US Patent and Trademark Office ("Official" US) – http://www.uspto.gov
Intellectual Property Network – www.patent.womplex.ibm.com
Patent Portal – www.vcilp.org/-rgrunner/patport.htm
Timestream, Inc., the Multimedia Publishers (reference material on intellectual property protection: 6114 LaSalle Avenue, Suite 300, Oakland, California, 94611 USA, 510-339-2463 Voice, 510-339-6469 Fax) – http://www.timestream.com.

done – but you have to register before you file an infringement suit, and registering early will make you eligible to receive attorney's fees and damages in a lawsuit.

Copyrights may be used to protect ads and product package designs when trademark protection is not applicable. A copyright owner has five exclusive rights:

- *Reproduction Right* – the right to copy, duplicate, or transcribe the work.

- *Modification Right* – the right to modify the work to create a new work. A new work that is based on a preexisting work is known as a "derivative work."

- *Distribution Right* – the right to distribute copies of the work to the public by sale, rental, lease, or lending.

- *Public Performance Right* – the right to recite, play, dance, act, or show the work at public place or to transmit it to the public. In the case of a movie, video or other AV work, showing the images in sequence is considered "performance." Some things, such as sound recordings, do not have a public performance right.

- *Public Display Right* – the right to show a copy of the work directly or by other means – film, slides, video, etc. to the public. In the case of a motion picture or other AV work, showing the images out of sequence is still considered "display."

Anyone who violates any of the exclusive rights of a copyright owner is called an infringer. Going after infringers is one of the ways to protect the valuable identity of a brand as represented by ads or packages, or literature/manuals, etc.

Make sure we know which of the "ideas" we may want to copy or use are protected by someone else's intellectual property rights. Otherwise we might invest a lot of time and money establishing a brand position in a name we cannot use.

The length of time of copyright protection depends on three factors:

- who created the work,

- when the work was created, and

- when it was first distributed commercially.

For US copyrighted works created on and after January 1, 1978, the term for those created by individuals is the life of the author plus 50 years. The copyright term for "works made for hire" is 75 years from the date of first "publication" (distribution of copies to the general public) or 100 years from the date of creation, whichever expires first. This term is currently the topic of a legal debate in the US. US Congress passed a new law extending it by 20 years, as of late 1998, but the constitutionality of this extension is currently being challenged.

Generally, the copyright is owned by the person (or persons) who created the work. However, if the work is created by employee as part of his or her employment, the employer owns the copyright because it results from a "work for hire." The copyright law also includes another form of "work for hire": it applies only to certain types of works which are specially commissioned works, for which an agreement was signed in advance.

You don't need a copyright license to copy facts from a protected work, because the copyright on a work does not extend to the work's facts.

A simple way to look at the alternatives

It may be helpful to think about the various forms of brand and brand name protection this way: the registered trademark actually protects your chosen brand name and/or icon, logo, etc. having used the trademark ahead of competitors, on the products and in the markets where it is intended to be registered can provide an edge in a contest as to who should have rights to a name, logo or icon. Copyrights can protect ads, tag lines, video images, etc. but are a much weaker type of protection and more easily circumvented.

Patent Law only applies in certain cases

Patent laws protect inventions and processes ("utility" patents) and ornamental designs ("design" patents). Inventions and processes protected by utility patents can be electrical, mechanical, or chemical in nature. Utility patents may protect a product or process, but take a long time to obtain and do not protect a brand name – even if the product is the virtual embodiment of what the brand name has come to mean to consumers. Design patents can be a useful part of the total "web" of protection, but like copyrights, are more easily circumvented by making relatively minor changes to the design. A more effective form of protection is provided in the trademark laws under section 43(a) of the Lanham Act. This portion deals with a confusingly similar appearance known as "trade dress" in which would cause a reasonable person to easily confuse the two products (or brand names/logos/icons).

The reason patents are time-consuming to obtain is that there are strict requirements for obtaining both utility and design patents. To qualify for a utility patent, an invention must be new, useful, and "non obvious" (the invention not have been obvious to a person having ordinary skill in that field). To meet the novelty requirement, the invention cannot have been

Sometimes the term "patent pending" is a greater deterrent than the actual issuance of a patent – especially because the contents of most applications are hidden until the patent issues. Competitors don't know what the pending patent protects, and may be hesitant to make large investments in fear of infringement.

known or used by others in this country and must not have been patented or described in a printed publication in the US or a foreign country before the applicant invented it. The policy behind the novelty requirement is that a patent is issued in exchange for the inventor's disclosure to the public of the details of his invention.

Protection under patents is more effective for products, but not usually appropriate for brand names alone. A patent holder can exclude others from making, using, or selling the patented invention/design in the US during the term of the patents life (17 years for utility patents and 14 for design patents). Anyone who makes, uses , or sells a patented item in the US during the term of the patent, and without permission from the patent owner is an infringer – even if they did not copy the patented invention or design – and even if they did not know about it. Once the patent on an invention or design has expired, anyone is free to make, use, or sell the invention or design.

Where other forms of protection don't work, trade secret laws may help.

In recent years, as workers have become more mobile, more employers have begun to appeal to trade secret laws to protect themselves from employees who leave and take critical competitive information to competitors. A trade secret is unique information of any kind that is valuable to its owner, that is not generally known, and that has been kept a secret by the owner. Trade secrets are protected only by state laws. The Uniform Trade

Secrets Act applies in a number of states and defines trade secrets as: "information, including a formula, pattern, compilation, program, device, method, technique, or process that derives independent economic value from not being generally known and not being readily ascertainable and is subject to reasonable efforts to maintain secrecy."

KILLER QUESTIONS

How can we retain people and protect our trade secrets from leaking to competitors?

Some typical kinds of material protected by the trade secret laws are: customer lists, instructional methods, manufacturing processes, and methods of developing software. Inventions and secret processes that are not patentable can often be protected under trade secret laws. Often patent applicants rely on trade secret law to protect inventions while patent applications are pending – which can be period of several years or more. It is not so clear exactly how trade secret laws apply to brands and branding, but market research and plans to launch a brand fit many of the criteria to be covered under trade secret laws.

There are six factors generally used as tests to determine whether particular information is a trade secret:

- extent to which the information is known outside the business

- extent to which the information is known by the employees

- extent of measures taken to guard the secrecy of the information

- value of the information to the claimant and its competitors

Smart things to say about brands

You usually know if you are taking trade secrets in your head when you take a job with a competitor, so proceed with caution. Lawsuits in this field are increasingly common.

- amount of effort or money expended developing the information

- ease with which the information could be acquired by others.

Trade secret protection is earned automatically when information of value to the owner is kept secret by the owner. Trade secret protection endures so long as the requirements for protection – generally, value to the owner and secrecy – continue to be met. The protection is lost if the owner fails to take reasonable steps to keep the information secret.

Use a brand as a brand, not as part of the language

Using a brand properly is a key to making it strong, protecting it and not letting it migrate over the line into the awful trap of losing the rights to it because it became a generic term and part of the language. Many well-known brands walk the line every day. Becoming so dominant that every cola ordered is a Coke, every copy requested is a Xerox, all the Christmas packages were sealed with Scotch Tape, and all premium shipments were FedEx'd can be the brand builder and marketer's delight and the intellectual property attorney's nightmare.

Brands must be portrayed as uniquely associated with a company's products or services, and when this wonderful, awful dominance starts to emerge, even more care must be taken. Thus 3M calls it Scotch Brand tape – even in ad copy and on packages – very intentionally and very wisely.

Smart things to say about brands

Use a brand name like a brand name, and not like a noun or a verb. Use it right or lose it! Choosing such an obvious name that it is a part of the language usually means you won't be able to protect it in the first place.

Generic names cannot be brands

Knowing how to choose a brand name that describes the product and can be protected is an important thing to know for a smart brand builder. A common mistake is to choose too generic a name in hopes of capturing the best possible brand. It usually doesn't work, or gets contested and the brand trademark disallowed after a lot has been invested in it. Names like "The Computer Store" and "Fresh Bread" are obvious, but not protectable. Commercial names like Super Glue and Windsurfer made a lot of sense to the companies that used them but not to intellectual property lawyers at the Patent and Trademark Office. Brand names need to be distinctive, not generic.

It is also illegal to confusingly mislead consumers as to the source or origin of things. Companies like McDonald's and Toys R Us have taken aggressive actions to protect the image of their brands. McHotel might be a cute name for a small, short-stay hotel, and McNewspaper might be a popular term for a *USA Today* type newspaper full of short, fast-to-read news items, but both infringe on McDonald's identity. A bike store named Bikes R Us would clearly infringe on the intellectual property rights of Toys R Us (who also sells bikes). Movies R Us as a video rental store would similarly raise legal issues based on the issue of similarity that is confusing to the consumer. The simplest rule to follow is "if you think you are stepping on someone's intellectual property, you probably are!" Only when there is the strongest of business reasons to do so is it even worth the effort to try – and then it is advisable to get the help of qualified legal counsel at the outset.

Once in a while, a reason so compelling exists for using a given brand name that the reward from winning a legal fight for it is worth the risk of losing and the cost/time it takes. This occurs when the previously mentioned common-law issue is on your side and someone else seems to have appropriated the brand just to keep it out of circulation after you have already invested heavily in using it for your product or service. In this kind of case, get an experienced, aggressive lawyer and be ready to spend some serious money. You could win back the rights to your brand!

8

Brand Management

WHAT IS BRAND MANAGEMENT AND WHAT DOES IT DO?

Someone must oversee that a brand is used properly, on products/packaging, or services, in advertising/promotion and this is especially the case if a product is distributed around the world in different cultures and using different languages.

Brand management

Good brand management is the most important factor in maintaining a brand's character, image and integrity. If you become a brand manager, you are entrusted with assets that are far more valuable than the company's buildings and equipment. These assets are the brands of a company that tell consumers what value to expect, and assure them that they are safe buying your brand – a brand they can trust. A table in an earlier chapter showed monetary values of a few of the most well-known brands. If you don't remember, Coke's brand was valued at almost $40 billion dollars – that is $40 million-million – and that is far more than the value of all but a handful of companies and a lot of small countries!

Brand management is very important

The brand managers that manage the Coke brand on a global basis have a huge job and tremendous responsibility. You probably recall that Procter & Gamble and Frito-Lay (division of Pepsico) are two of the world's best brand-management companies. Brand management is reputed to differ from other departments at P&G. It is far more intense, far more competitive and staffed only by the best and brightest that survive P&G's rigorous selection process. The same applies at Frito-Lay's Texas headquarters.

Every P&G CEO has come up through the brand management ranks since the system was put into use in the early 1930s. Graduates of the brand management system fill almost 90% of the company's management positions. In the US, P&G offer eight different laundry detergent brands, six bar-soap brands, four shampoo brands, three brands of toothpaste, and two fabric softeners, and that is in the US alone – and the list is constantly evolving. Each of the brands has a clearly delineated image and character, which differentiates it not only from competitors but also from other brands of the same product type.

How brand management works

When R&D or New Product Development creates a product, it is assigned to a brand manager, whose job it is to ensure the brand's success. Your

Smart quotes

primary challenge if you are a brand manager at companies like P&G, Frito-Lay, and others who effectively use brand management, is a battle for resources against other products and their brand managers! Unless a new product gets the attention and resources it needs, it may not make it – and after a couple of these, the brand manager will not make it either.

Since all of the brands in the company's stable are competing for a share of the same resources, brand managers must be forceful advocates and good internal sales representatives for their brand and its new products. A lot of your success depends on how well you have done your homework. Listening to consumers and documenting what they say and want is a key part of the brand manager's job, as is the constant internal sales pitch for resources. Because of this, brand managers spend a lot of time studying customers, analyzing market research data, observing consumer behavior, and finding the answers to what it is that consumers and customers find to be the best value.

Smart things to say about brands

Brand management is tough, rewarding duty, reserved for the best and the brightest. If you can't stand the heat, stay out of the kitchen!

Because of the heavy competition, brand management is a tough job, and brand managers must be unusually resilient. Good brand managers understand that they must follow the rules but occasionally, they must know when to break the rules and make new rules. In this context, brand man-

agers do not work in isolation. They must rely on support from people in other departments over whom they have no authority, and from whom other brand managers are also requesting help. The successful brand manager must find out what consumers and customers want, sell the importance of their product versus all of the other competing new products in their company and then muster the resources – people and money needed – to give their product its best chance at commercial success.

Even P&G make mistakes occasionally. When they entered the Japanese market, they did so with Cheer, a detergent that is noted to work equally well in hot, warm or cold water. Unfortunately this benefit was of not interest to the Japanese who predominantly use cold water for their laundry needs. They made this error because there was not enough knowledge of Japanese cultural habit, so P&G hired Japanese nationals into their

Smart quotes

- Consumers buy products but choose brands.
- Gorilla brands are better than guerilla brands.
- Expand benefits without compromising brands.
- Manage each brand as a separate business.
- Create global brands.
- The package is the face of the brand.
- Start a good commercial with a "Hey you!"
- Show the package in the first eight seconds.
- Link the brand to the story of the commercial.
- Rules are for the obedience of fools and the guidance of wise brand managers.

Charles L. Decker, *Winning with the P&G 99 – 99 Principles and Practices of Procter & Gamble's Success* (Pocket Books division of Simon & Schuster, 1998)

brand management, used a Japanese ad agency, and did Japanese focus groups and product tests before re-entering the market. They listened to the local customers and learned. When they next launched Cheer into Japan, it was formulated to take advantage of every opportunity they had identified – and it succeeded.

The evolution of brand management into category management

You find yourself in the midst of the most dramatic change in brand management over the past two decades. So what can you do? Become an expert on category management. One of the major developments in the past decade has been the emergence of category management. Whereas brand management deals with all of the aspects of a particular brand, it has more of an inside-out focus. Brand management takes an inside-the-company viewpoint and seeks to maximize the brand's share, position and equity through managerial effort.

In category management you take the outside-in view. Category management is the discipline by which a single supplier (or a small group of suppliers with a "category captain") manages the shelf space in a retail store. Category managers determine the number of facings of a product, the adjacencies of products and even product families in a section of a retail store. Category managers also have a strong influence in pricing, promotion, advertising and all of the marketing and sales activities for their category – which may encompass one or several brands. Category managers often control the placement and promotion of competing brands which are not as strong as their own brand, and thus have considerable power in the distribution channel where they work. Retail store management must carefully and firmly manage the efforts of category managers or they can lose control of their own store shelves.

In the modern world of business, it is useless to be a creative original thinker unless you can also sell what you create. Management cannot be expected to recognize a good idea unless it is presented to them by a good salesman.

David M. Ogilvy (founder Ogilvy & Mather advertising agency)

Category captains have similar roles in which they may do quasi-category management for retailers who are not ready or willing to relinquish to degree of control normally given to category managers, but want many of the merchandising and presentation/promotional benefits. This role of a category captain is also influential and can create a preeminent position for one supplier of what may be several competing brands. Done properly, using these category captains can take a load off the retail store merchandising staff – but careful monitoring of the category captains is still critical – lest the store management abdicate control of their own floor to suppliers.

KILLER QUESTIONS

How influential are we willing to let our category managers be?

Whereas brand management considers the performance of the brand itself, category management considers the performance of the entire category – including the competitive interaction of various purchase options that are on a retail display. As a category manager, you would typically expect to be responsible for the sales, profitability, inventory productivity, and merchandising/packaging of the entire category of products. In this way, you approximate the brand manager's role, but acting on behalf of your customer instead of your own company – which is the supplier. Some companies even use independent third parties for category managers. These might be distributors of the products, sales representatives who represent a leading product supplier or independent specialist consultants – who do the category management for both suppliers and retailers.

Brand management yields power to Sales Management and Customer Teams

Another development that has reduced the influence of brand managers is the growth of power in the hands of Sales Management, particularly with the advent of Customer Teams that service large influential customers. Wal*Mart, the world's largest retailer, is the premier example of a retailer where customer teams, often located in proximity to the Wal*Mart headquarters in Arkansas (US), have grown tremendously in influence. There are so many of these teams in Wal*Mart's Bentonville, AR headquarters area, that Wal*Mart is trying to determine how to slow or arrest their growth. These teams are having too great an influence on the Wal*Mart staff due to their proximity – both professionally and socially within the community.

KILLER QUESTIONS

Who is the champion of this brand, and how powerful is s/he?

Procter & Gamble were among the first major branded products company to adopt these powerful cross-functional teams and relocate them to the customer's home-town area. This created an inevitable tension between

Smart quotes

There is a need for inter-functional coordination between Brand management and Sales management due to the increasing emphasis on partnering and relationship marketing. Organizational changes such as downsizing and restructuring have a significant impact on inter-functional relationships (including dysfunctional conflict) as well as on job attitudes of affected managers.

Dr Richard C. Reizenstein

sales management, customer service staff, forecasting/logistics, and brand management located together at the customer's site. No longer was the brand manager the controlling function. The power shifted to the sales managers who led the customer teams.

Customer partnerships and relationship marketing transferred the primary role to the sales management function. This does not mean that brand management was not important any more. It does mean that brand oriented roles were less influential in the overall decision making process and strategies that result. Brand management's role was also dramatically impacted by widespread downsizing, consolidation of functions, changes in the span of control, and consolidation, which created these powerful mega-customers. Even though the technical roles may have diffused and blurred, the brand issues that must be faced remain largely the same. They are just located in different sets of functionally named units.

Other issues raised by such brand management diffusion are those of compensation comparisons between sales management and brand management personnel, forecasting control between sales, brand management and logistics, and last but perhaps most of all, communications gaps related to the power struggle that inevitably occurs. This area is still in a state of flux, and the final outcome is not clear. The amazing growth of Internet selling and marketing will only muddle things further. Suffice it to say, "Brand management ain't what it used to be!"

SMART VOICES

The leader is always a target, so if you say you're going to do something, you'd better do it. That is the brand leader's responsibility.

George Sine, Jr. (Director of Marketing – Worldwide, Titleist Golf Balls)

Balancing the Short Term with the Long Term is a Challenge

One of the most difficult tasks faced by a brand manager and the senior executive ranks in any branded product company is the conflict between short and long term results. Wall Street pressures for sales and earnings growth quarter after quarter, year after year can present serious dilemmas for brand managers. Advertising is usually one of the largest pots of discretionary spending in any consumer products company. Too often it is viewed as "expense" money instead of "investment" money. Expense money can remain unspent to prop up earnings in a lackluster quarter, and the resultant consequences are fairly evident – something did not get done because it was not funded.

Unfortunately, when advertising in support of a brand is the "expense" that is postponed, the consequences may not show up immediately but may be far more serious than is often realized.

Brand names take years to build in the mind of the consumer. Unfortunately as new brands flood into the market, all with ads screaming for consumers' attention, the older brands come under siege. Only if those brands receive consistent support in advertising and promotion can they hold their own against the new upstarts. Once a brand is established, it is all too easy to fall into the trap of saving money, or increasing profits and earnings per share by forgoing planned advertising. What a devastating error this is.

> Without a decent short term, there is no long term. Pay attention to results each quarter, while trying not to sacrifice the long term for the short term. If you always make the quarter, you always make the year!

Smart things to say about brands

In an earlier chapter, I mentioned Titleist golf balls and their premium brand position, which is accompanied with a premium price position. It is appropriate to revisit the Titleist story here, where we are talking about consistency in what a brand stands for. George Sine, Jr. is the Director of Marketing for Golf Balls, Worldwide for Titleist. I spoke with him at length about the "smart things" Titleist does to sustain their preeminent brand position.

George's comments were insightful and centered around a theme that would be wise for all brand management and marketing management to heed. George said, "We don't bring a product to market until we've proven it delivers on what we promised – we believe in continuously delivering performance even better than the golfer expects, no matter what their skill level, from touring pro to weekend golfer."

That is a bold statement, but one which Titleist obviously backs up, judging from their success. They are the brand image leader, and the market share leader. In fact, very recently, 15 straight US PGA tournament winners were playing Titleist balls. Of course Titleist pays pros to use their balls, but the pros would not use a product that put them at a competitive disadvantage. There is simply too much prize money at stake.

As I discussed further how Titleist ensures the integrity of the brand, we moved to the topic of price competition. George commented, "other brands may try to shift share by using price or promotional money, but we rely on product performance." Example: The Titleist Tour Distance ball: these come in a blue box for those readers who are familiar with Titleist's famous black box for Tour Balata (professional's choice) and red box for their DT (weekend golfers' choice) packaging. The Tour Distance came from their desire to provide the more skilled amateur with a ball that had much of the spin performance used by pros to "control the ball" and the added distance amateurs often treasure. Thus the Tour Distance was born and in just a couple short years, became its best selling ball. It was true to their brand's proposition – the best performance – period!

Titleist's philosophy of using a combination of experience and technological know-how to make the best golf balls originated with founder Phil Young's golfing experiences. Young was playing golf with a competitor's ball one day, and noticed that even well-struck shots seemed to be going awry. He became suspicious about the balls and took them back to the lab for x-ray examination. The balls were off center – meaning the inside was not concentric with the outside.

Young took steps to ensure that Titleist balls were as accurately made as technology permitted. Titleist uses several kinds of construction to provide different performance characteristics, whereas most of their competitors use a single process and attempt to vary material parameters to offer differing performance – solid multi-layer balls for one kind of performance, wound-liquid center balls for another, and so forth.

The purpose of this level of detail is to illustrate that being a brand leader means more than just telling a good story in ads and promotions. As George Sine so aptly puts it, "The leader's job is to meet and then exceed the expectation of the players who use the product – and to provide an equipment advantage."

Titleist goes to considerable lengths to avoid sullying its leading brand name by getting into price wars, or cutting corners on quality and performance. It employs two different brands to combat the price discounters and the mid-price performance-claim competitors. Pinnacle is the discount brand, which is sold to less skilled players. For this market, the ball is made to be very durable and go a long way – the two major desires of the less skilled player. Spin, a characteristic valued by touring pros is the curse of the weekend player because it makes hooks or slices more extreme – so the ball has a low spin rate by intent. The Cobra brand, named after Titleist's popular King Cobra club product line, is a mid-price performance ball with balanced features to compete with Nike, Spalding, Wilson, etc. These two brands let Titleist do battle in price-sensitive markets without undermining the premium position of their premier brand.

The final comments George made really hit home on brand image and consistency. "The leader is always a target, so if you say you're going to do something, you'd better do it. That is the brand-leader's responsibility."

Brand mangers must fight like crazed warriors to support and build their brand, especially if it is a strong leader. Once a brand is the leader, there is only one way for it to go – down. Diverting advertising and promotion that is intended to support a brand for the purpose of supporting short-term earnings is a sure route to disaster. Just as failing to maintain a critical piece of production machinery is foolish economy, so also is starving a successful brand of the support it needs to remain strong.

Consistency in brand identity is important

There are two schools of thought on this topic. One says, "always

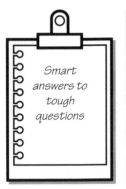
Q: How do companies harm their brand image by their choice of icons and themes?

A: An example is a good way to illustrate what damage a lack of consistent style and image can do to a brand. It is easy for well-intended efforts to portray the brand in either a less desirable quality of representation, or in totally outlandish ways.

IBM was always noted for their strait-laced conformance to corporate image. Thus it makes an excellent example when it does something far from that conformance. When IBM was going through its tough times before Louis Gerstner took over, there was a case where an IBM ad actually portrayed the brand with a picture of an eye, a picture of a bee, and a large block M. Does this fit your image of IBM – or of a local day care center?

IBM is about leadership, information solutions and high technology, not about picture puzzles that communicate the brand. This kind of misuse of brand icons and images was stopped firmly in recent years. IBM's legendary brand is recovering quite nicely now. The more recent e-commerce ads, on the other hand, treat the IBM logo, blue color, image and identity wonderfully.

present your brand in a consistent manner, using the same icons, typography styles, etc." The other one says, "get exposure wherever, however you can." That view is dangerous. Most companies have a style guide – either formal or informal – controlled by the marketing, advertising or brand management people. This is a good idea.

Some experts contend that rigidly enforcing things like styles of documents and typography are foolish and restrict creativity. I disagree. There is a apparent unspoken quality about graphic works that are done consistently and tastefully. Unless the image of the brand is one of crazy, mixed-up, off-the-wall products, the style needs to be consistent. If it is an eclectic or off-beat image, then the style needs to avoid being consistent. Doing either one well requires effort, thought and communication of how the desired result is to be achieved.

THE CHAMPION OF BRAND CONSISTENCY

The Marlboro Man – the consistent image has grown and been successful for decades. Marlboro has historically been the best selling cigarette outside the US, especially in heavy user Pacific rim markets. The Marlboro brand image as portrayed by the Marlboro Man, the ad settings and the ad theme "Come to where the flavor is. Come to Marlboro Country" have been amazingly consistently managed and successful. A line of products reminiscent of the rough-and-tumble life in Marlboro country reinforces the brand imagery. A very limited amount of brand extension has kept the image free of confusion. Even with no US TV or radio advertising, and as far back as 1992, Marlboro was spending over $100,000,000 in advertising to support this powerful brand franchise.

SMART VOICES

Building a great brand depends on knowing the right stuff. Eight brand-building principles of great brands were identified by Scott Bedbury in *Fast Company* magazine. Bedbury helped build the Nike brand name and is now helping build Starbucks. Pretty heady credentials, and well deserved it seems. Consider these brand building principles carefully:

1. A great brand is in it for the long haul.
2. A great brand can be anything. Some categories may lend themselves to branding better than others, but anything is brandable.
3. A great brand knows itself. Anyone who wants to build a great brand first has to understand who they are.
4. A great brand invents or reinvents an entire category.
5. A great brand taps into emotions.
6. A great brand is a story that's never completely told.
7. A great brand has design consistency.
8. A great brand is relevant.

These principles are elaborated in *Fast Company* (issue10 p. 96), or: http://www.fastcompany.com

The job of brand management is to be certain that these eight principles are never far from the minds of top management and working levels alike. Not an easy task, but an essential one for success in brand management.

9

Private Brands

IS THE THREAT OF PRIVATE LABEL AND GENERIC BRANDS SERIOUS?

Private label, house brands and generics are all threats to brand names since they offer an alternative to the consumer, usually with a different value proposition, often at a lower price. How can private brands undermine a recognized brand? Easily, if not managed well! Dual branding as a strategy has risks and rewards.

Private brands

Will national or global brands be eclipsed by private brands?

In an earlier chapter I covered the highlights of private labels and store brands. I did that to put them into perspective in the topic where they fit.

There is much more to know about private brands, so here's a short chapter to fill in the gaps.

The debate rages on every decade or so that private brands, the province of the mega-retailers, will sound the death-knell for national or global brands. How ridiculous that argument sounds in 1999. It was only a few short years ago that the popular opinion among many experts was that premium brands were doomed. These high-priced alternatives would be eclipsed by high-value generic or private brands that performed as well, looked as good and cost a lot less.

The debate on the future strength of private labels (or store brands) ebbs and flows with economic conditions. When the economy is good, national or global brands, usually selling at premium prices, reign supreme. When the economy is uncertain or in a decline, private labels, store brands or even generic brands gain in strength – usually because they are more competitively priced. What is the truth? Is there a decline in national or global brands in favor of store or private brands?

KILLER QUESTIONS

Will our customers knock-off our brand with private labels or house brand lookalikes – and how fast?

I won't keep you in suspense – the decline and demise of such widely known and respected brands didn't happen and never will. In fact, you will find national and global brands are probably stronger than ever because of the proliferation of private labels and store brands. Competition forced national brands to sharpen their pricing, but most of all to clarify their focus. Store brands will likely always be with us. It is a way for a retailers to duck competition on highly advertised products and/or create differentiation – one of the key values of brands in the first place.

Sears has been notorious – both notoriously successful with brands like Kenmore and Craftsman – and notorious for wanting to duck

Do shoppers know what they're going to buy before they enter a store? The answer is yes and no. A customer has an idea of the products and services desired, but not until in the store does a shopper make the decision to buy. The Point of Purchase Advertising Institute verifies this, stating in their consumer buying-habits study that over 70% of all buying decisions are made in the store.

Ideations – concepts in retail (the Newsletter of Design Forum, Dayton, OH, Winter 1999).

head-to-head competition with retailers like Wal*Mart, Kmart, Target, Home Depot, and Lowe's. Sears' cost structure and overhead due to mall store locations and corporate infrastructure make it difficult or impossible for them to compete with these "big box" general merchandise discounters. What do they do? They show national brands at good prices, and then surround them with their own brands at better, albeit more profitable prices.

Sears have come a long way in the past decade, especially in their Brand Central appliance and electronics area. It is almost competitive – but not quite. Ed Brennan was at the helm of Sears when this branded-product initiative took shape. Just as his younger brother Bernie Brennan had done at Montgomery Ward with Electric Avenue a few years earlier, Sears expanded their assortment to offer their shoppers the popular brand-name appliances, TV, etc. that they wanted to buy. National brands were the "must have" to give their departments credibility as a full line place to shop for key items.

Private labels and store brands as competitive tools

This is why national and global brands will continue not only to survive but also to prosper. These highly recognized brands may be loss leaders

> **Smart things to say about brands**

When using private brands or store brands, make sure there are clear value trade-offs in price, features and performance. Consumers won't choose them unless they understand these tradeoffs.

when Sears or Wards choose to promote them, but the "loss" is at least equally in the store's margins as it is in the manufacturer's.

When the store becomes the brand

Store labels provide differentiation and another tier of value for shopper. In days gone by, Sears were known for their "Good, Better, Best" merchandising. This allowed the consumer to have a choice – a trade-off-in features and price. Controlling the specifications of an entire line of private- or store-branded products makes rationalization of lines like this a lot more convenient. Mervyns; Kenmore & Craftsman; Wal*Mart's Old Roy and Better Homes & Gardens/Popular Mechanics are all store brands derived from either the name of the store, the name of magazines, names created from ideas of merchants or the name of Sam Walton's old hunting dog.

Each one of these is a powerful brand in terms of sales. The retailers who sell them made them powerful by their promotional spending, advertising and/or retail shelf space. This was not without purpose. The store brand was only available at their store. No competitive retailer could offer or promote it. This makes comparison shopping much more difficult for consumers, and makes establishing brand value much more controllable by retailers.

You will find different branded manufacturers are all trying to outdo each other, and thus they vary the specifications and features to meet the price points and margins they want to hit at retail. Mix in four or five national brands and logical, step-by-step value schemes go out the window. One brand may have a better image – like Sony – and choose to only offer higher price point goods. Another like Panasonic or Magnavox may choose to cover all of the value steps, while a low-end competitor like Samsung or Sanyo may only offer products at lower price tiers.

Exclusive distribution networks

There are situations occurring with increasing frequency where the store is not only the brand but also the only place where the products are available. This form of exclusive distribution of a brand and a store name can be a very powerful combination. A good example is Anita Roddick's popular "Body Shop" stores. The products in those stores are exclusively their own brands, which they create, manage, and distribute as well as retail. The benefit is total control of the brand – pricing, promotion, display and distribution. The penalty is that the retailer has to do all of those jobs and still make enough margin to pay for all of people in those functions.

US direct marketers Land's End and L.L. Bean have a similar level of control, and responsibility. So does the famous Victoria's Secrets stores and catalogs. Who says sex doesn't sell? What are they really selling? Underwear and nighties, or thinly veiled voyeurism and titillation? The answer? Who cares – if they sell the goods, build the brand and make money! They own and control the distribution chain for their brand from end to end.

> Exclusive means no one else has it or can have it – we must use exclusives carefully. Give them sparingly. Create them wisely. Once done they are hard to undo. Once undone, they are nearly impossible to re-establish.

Smart things to say about brands

The recent spate of outlet stores and outlet malls along US interstate highways have created another form of captive or semi-captive retail outlets. Polo-Ralph Lauren and Tommy Hilfiger brands are sold at premium prices in department store boutiques, and in their own stand-alone mall stores.

At the outlet centers, both sell limited parts of their product assortments, blemished goods, overstocks, and extra production runs at prices 40–50% below the premium outlets.

Housewares makers Corning Ware and Rubbermaid are national brands also found in the Outlet Malls spaced just far enough (40–50 miles, 65–90 km) from major retail centers to avoid incurring the wrath of their major customers. Over time, consumers will decide how such outlets affect their view of brands and value. As they do, the brands may lose some of their cachet and exclusivity by virtue of being available at much lower prices if consumers are willing to drive an hour each way. This is a threat to the brand's equity and the value trade-off of extra sales volume vs. lower brand image is a risky one.

House brands can duck competition – sort of

Retailers can duck competition to some extent by introducing a "house brand" like those listed earlier in this chapter. They can offer brands that no one else can offer. These brands can offer unique feature and price combinations, so the retailers can then "cherry-pick" the national brands to provide value references for their own brands. It has worked in the past for Sears and Wards, and it is working now for Wal*Mart, Target, Kmart, Home Depot and Lowe's.

Consumers usually buy brands because they can trust the brand to provide a reliable package of value. If the store can trade on its reputation, it can transfer that trust to its own brand of products. When this strategy is coupled with liberal return, exchange or warranty policies, the consumer risk is greatly reduced. They know Wal*Mart will stand behind the Popular Mechanics tools or Better Homes and Gardens home products they sell in their stores. After all, these are familiar names being sold at the most popular place to shop in the world.

Target stores takes a slightly different approach – perhaps one that is more rooted in their department store heritage as part of Dayton-Hudson Corporation, and sister division to Mervyn's – one of the pioneer "all-store brand" chains. Target employs style and design consultants as part of their merchandising staff to be sure that their clothing brands, like Cherokee, Honors and others, are in style and suitably fashion forward for the tastes of their targeted shoppers.

Segmenting markets with "fighting brands"

Who would have imagined that powerhouse companies would begin to introduce their own secondary brands to preserve the brand cachet of their primary brand. This is exactly what Hewlett-Packard is doing as they introduced the Apollo brand for printers. HP has not sold its own name-brand printers in the price range of $100 and lower – and does not want to! Thus they create what is often called a "fighting brand". A "fighting brand" is a brand created to fight price battles, and used by a brand leader who wants to protect the price premiums normally associated with the image of its brand.

When the path of obvious attack for sales of a branded product is blocked so thoroughly that it fails to open up to even the most valiant efforts, find a way around the obstacle – like another brand that can be licensed.

HP currently controls about half of the overall ink-jet printer market, and hopes that the Apollo brand will capture about the same share of the under-$100 market. The challenge HP will face is a daunting one – identifying Apollo with HP as its parent without dragging the premium-priced HP brand down with the cheaper, lower specification (and performance) Apollo brand.

This strategy has met with only mixed success in the past. Samsonite luggage tried this with the American Tourister brand, after American Tourister tried itself to use dual brand, fighting-brand strategies. The outcome was unclear, but not a resounding success. More likely what resulted was a subdivision of the market on distribution and price but without clear brand-segmentation benefits.

How Private and Store Brands co-exist with well-known brands

Selling store brands or private brands is a common phenomenon in the supermarket and pharmacy. Nearly all the major grocery and drug chains have their own brands of the most popular items. These items are usually displayed in proximity to the major brand items. The packages are usually similar in coloration and styling – at least as much as is possible without violating the trade dress sections of the Lanham act.

The growth in large store chains is a phenomenon occurring in both the US and major European markets. In the US, discount-store chains

BIGGER GROCERY CHAINS = MORE BUYING POWER

Percentage market share held by the Top Five largest grocery chains:

Country	1988	1996
Britain	53%	64%
France	42%	52%
Germany	28%	40%
Spain	19%	25%

The Economist, 10 April 1999, p.76

Wal*Mart, Kmart and Target hold over 70% of all general merchandise discount sales. This consolidation of large store chains creates a powerful buying influence, making the acquisition cost of store brands lower than would be normally the case. European chains show largely the same sort of picture. The chart above shows the European grocery industry consolidation of power that leads to the potential for ever more powerful store branded goods.

The store brand is virtually always lower in price or offers a larger quantity at the same price. By placing the items close to the major name brands, packaging them in similar looking cartons or containers, the stores are actually helping the consumer see the value that is added by the name brand. No one knows if the contents of the packages are really different or the same. Are they made by the same company on the same production line? Only the brand name is clearly why the cost is different. By

KILLER QUESTIONS

Is our price premium holding up a price umbrella that invites private brands into the market, and should we develop fighting brands of our own?

virtue of the brand name's equity, image, identity and reputation alone, consumers pay higher prices for what may be the same product.

Few cases more clearly illustrate the drawing power and value of brands better than this one. If consumers actually buy both products and try them, they may perceive a difference, or they may not! In the case of non-prescription pain relievers or cold remedies, it may be virtually impossible to detect the difference. In that case, the store brand may win the next and future purchases. In the cases of cereal, jellies, coffee or vegetables, there may be a perceptible difference. Whether the store brand is better or worse may even be debatable – but it is perceptibly different, and in this case, the brand name wins. Why? Because the widely recognized brand is the benchmark, it gets to define how its product should taste or work or feel. This is another key benefit of major brand names selling next to generics, store brand or private labels.

SMART VOICES

A NEW LOOK FOR AN OLD STORE BRAND

It seems that Steve Goubeaux of Visual Marketing Associates (VMA) and Tim Horne of CharBroil collaborated on another brand/style differentiation project that was a big success. Sears had been struggling to fight price competition with their Kenmore brand of gas grills for some time. Everyone's grills look so much alike that consumers couldn't find the value differences to support Sears' premium pricing structure. Through a collaborative design effort, VMA and CharBroil came up with a distinctively new and unique Sears look and feature package. As Steve tells it, "of all the styles tested, their recommendation to Sears was to take the most radically new looking one – a risk to be certain – but the reward of a longer period of unique appeal in a time of dramatically shrinking product life-cycles." The result – CharBroil won the lion's share of Sears' business with the new design and Sears could offer a really unique value proposition to its consumers. The store brand was now truly different from the national brands.

Gas and charcoal grill manufacturer CharBroil uses a multi-brand strategy to sell competing retailers similar products will different cosmetics, labels, specifications and assortments. Only a decade ago, CharBroil was struggling as the number 2 or 3 grill maker, having been displaced from the top spot by Sunbeam barbecue grills on the strength of Sunbeam's sales to Wal*Mart and Wal*Mart's incredible growth. None of the big three discounters nor Sears wanted to go head-to-head on the same products. The solution was simple: brand segmentation by retailer. Wal*Mart bought Sunbeam, Kmart bought CharBroil, and Target bought Thermos brand grills. Sears sold its own brand, and stayed out of the fray that way.

> *Smart quotes*
>
> The ultimate irony – you have to offer another brand name to let the retailer compete with your own brand name!
>
> Steve Goubeaux (Partner, Visual Marketing Associates)

A multi-brand strategy can break down barriers and open new opportunities. Tim Horne is CEO of Char-Broil, a division of the W.C. Bradley Co. and also serves as President, W.C. Bradley Co. Home Leisure Group. Tim relates a story about the power of a brand that effected millions of dollars of business at a mass retail customer. "For years we had been trying to sell to one of the big three discounters with absolutely no luck. We were selling to the other two, but number three was not about to buy our product because we sold to their competition."

These big retailers are very sensitive about differentiation from each other, and a brand is a key differentiator. Tim continued, "Each year this retailer suffered with a lack of product innovation in the category, poor comparative product quality, and bad service, all for the privilege of having a distinctive brand on their sales floor. This retailer even endured a major product recall, which cost the company millions of dollars in lost sales and negative consumer relations and they still wouldn't buy from us!

Who says brands are not powerful motivators – even at the retailer buyer level? As we talked further, Tim described the lengths to which they went to overcome this objection about brands. "We offered them industry leading innovation, excellent quality, competitive prices, and outstanding service and we were still on the outside looking in. A brand name alone held us hostage at this retailer in spite of all the hard work that we had done to build a world class business. Finally, I determined that our only option to ever sell this retailer would come down to resolving the brand name issue. For this retailer all else appeared to be secondary."

CharBroil's struggle to penetrate this brand segmentation was epic, as they ran into obstacle after obstacle – including the large discount store chains' mutual animosity toward each other. The solution – introduce another brand – finally worked. This strategy of introducing a "fighting brand" – even though it was not a "low price fighting brand" which they often are – let CharBroil grow until they have now reclaimed the leadership position in the industry. Once this rigid retailer brand segmentation mentality was broken down, the individual brands once again competed on the merits of their offerings instead of simply who carried which brand.

When the consumer is "bribed" to buy the store brand

Many large store chains have begun offering their own brand of products with a "club-like" discount. Consumers must sign up and then present a bar-coded ID tag or membership card to get these discounts. These retailers have also decided to overcome consumer resistance to their house brands by offering full replacement guarantees with national/name branded equivalents. It is obvious that the brand value and the profit difference is significant if the retailer will go to these extremes to incite consumers to try their store brand products.

Who can you trust – and what brand can you trust?

Trust is the ultimate characteristic that makes brands valuable. Trust may reside in the reputation of the manufacturer; or trust may be placed in the reputation of the retail store. Whichever of these factors adds the trust factor to the brand, significant value is added. In small stores with proprietors who own and work in the store, the proprietor may recommend the product and confer his own trust element to that product or brand. Wherever it comes from – trust in a relatively unknown brand is the basis for the success of all private brand, store label or non-name branded products and services.

KILLER QUESTIONS

Are we willing to co-brand or sub-brand with customers?

Conclusion

The Future of Branding

WHAT MIGHT BRAND NAMES BECOME IN THE FUTURE?

As information-overload grows, and the time to process it shrinks, signals provided by brands increase in importance, and change the brands' very nature, because they save information-processing time, and direct consumers to specific options in making decisions. As categories blur, so will brands. How mergers affect brands is critical. But brands are the keys to success in the future.

Anything, anytime, anywhere – "there is no there, there is only here and we are all here!"

The quotation: "There is no *there*, there is only *here* and we are all here!" comes from an MCI network ad of several years ago, long before it became part of WorldCom and could really deliver on the promise. Academy award-winning child actress Anna Pacquin is pictured in various and obviously different geographical settings. She reminds us that the power of the network to move information at the speed of light makes it possible for everyone to be interconnected wherever they are. This power is now almost a global reality thanks to satellite communications.

Think about it. You can now buy almost anything you want, anywhere you want, anytime you want, without leaving the comfort of your home, your office, your car or your vacation or business trip and have it delivered to your home or office (or anywhere else you specify) within a day or two. What comes next? "Beaming" products or people like the "transporter" in the famous TV series StarTrek is still far off. But computers and phones that accept voice commands are here. Motorola's StarTac phone is almost a copy of the StarTrek communicator. Nokia's 6000 series lets you not only use a phone but also connect to the Internet, surf, do email, and more. Nextel's system lets users within confined ranges communicate like they had personal communicators with them, yet make phone calls anywhere in an instant.

Want to choose the news topics you receive via the web, the stock prices in your portfolio, the weather in the cities you specify, and today's horo-

Smart quotes

Permission marketing

Traditional advertising is interruptive. With interactive advertising, the goal is to reward customers for their attention and get them to act of their own free will.

James Ryan, "How to Be a Prize Fighter," *Business 2.0*, May 1999

scope? No problem – it comes up now as your home page when you sign onto the web. With every one of these technological innovations comes some form of advertising – for brands. Banners come up much faster than web pages do. Brands scroll across the screen, pop up in windows, change colors, and do all sort of things to get your attention. Brands are created in weeks or months that used to take years and decades. Some of them fade and die just as quickly. Where is all of this going? What does it mean to brands and branding? Well, hang on and lets take a supersonic ride to the future of brands and branding that you are going to have to cope with, cave-in to, or capitalize on.

There are two fundamental kinds of transaction done on the Internet. One is business-to-consumer, and the other is business-to-business. The economic models are quite different in how each must make money. Brands are important in both models, but in different ways. Business-to-consumer actually sells a product or service and, if they do it right, get paid more for it than it costs to acquire and deliver. Herein lies the problem. Some brands have made their name by selling a huge variety of products very cheap (like amazon.com does with books and music CDs). Many others sell at

The Web is influencing people's feelings about brands, according to *Online Branding, The Internet's Impact on Branding*, a study from Cyber Dialogue. The study found 36% of Internet users say that their opinions of one or more product brands have changed as a result of using the Internet. The study also found that "brand impressionable" users are more likely to shop online and offline. The study also reported the Internet can increase store traffic, direct-mail purchases and TV shopping.

Advertising Age, December 1998 (copyright Crain Communications Inc.)

Smart things to say about brands

cost or even give products away in hopes of making money on ancillary services like "selling eyeballs". Some of these Internet retailers collect for sales before required to pay for the products. This "negative working capital" model lets them survive on cash flow in the absence of profitable transactions. All are betting on some form of future profit sources to be found before the cash flow runs out.

Here is where the brand issue becomes important. The Internet term, "selling eyeballs," describes the idea of attracting as many people to a web site just as TV programs hope to attract the most viewers. That traffic will then (they hope) become attractive to advertisers, and generate enough income to sustain their "giveaways." Maybe the address list of visitors can be sold for a profit, but whether this model of brand advertising and promotion is inherently profitable enough to be economically viable remains to be seen. Thus far, only America Online and Yahoo! (of the well-known Internet portals/brand names) have found formulas for making real profit. The other sites live off cash flow and cheap capital raised from venture capitalists and inflated stock price offerings.

Business-to-business Internet commerce follows a different model. Selling products, information, services, etc., is an economically viable use of the Internet for business-to-business transactions. Whether brands become important in this arena depends on how the transactions are managed. The destination web site has the potential to become a brand in itself (Purchasing networks are the best example of this type). Or, the service or product provider may become the dominant brand in the web surfer's mind. In some cases both may become important brands. This is a new profit-making business model already, and

KILLER QUESTIONS

How fast can we get our brand to market and how can we use the Information Infrastructure (e.g. Internet, telecommunications, computers, networks, etc.) to accelerate that process?

Smart quotes

I think brands are *more important than ever* because of the Internet!

Jack Kahl (CEO, Manco, Inc.)

when many sites offer near equivalent services, trusted brands will determine the winners and losers.

The brands and shoppers of the future

Web TV turns the your TV set into an Internet surfer. Laptops at fewer than 3 pounds or less are common. Other laptop computers have the power and memory of mainframes of just decade ago. Want to know anything, find anything, and do anything? Check it out on the web. It's probably there. Don't like shopping? "Someone" will shop for you – or more likely a "bot" will shop for you. A "bot" is short for a robot shopper that is an intelligent agent which will search the Internet for whatever brand you want, compare prices and availability, and offer several choices. This shopping method is not yet fully refined yet, but the process and technology are there and being used, and brands are the premier search parameters.

Is this an important issue to you in the future of brands and branding? You better believe it is. The bot will look for the brand you specify – if you specify one. If no brand is specified, how will you tell your bot what you want? Generic descriptions might work for a loaf of whole-wheat bread or a gallon of skim milk, but what about clothing, appliances, personal care items and billions of other choices. Brands are not just an important part of the future – they are the keys to success in the future.

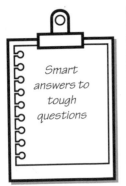

Q: How big is the traffic on the Internet?

A: It is huge and still growing, but has week-to-week variations, and growth seems to leveling off to a lower rate.

Top Twenty Web digital media sites, week of April 11–17, 1999

	Site	Number of visitors
1.	AOL Network	47,009,000
2.	Microsoft sites	31,994,000
3.	Lycos	31,915,000
4.	Yahoo	31,272,000
5.	Go Network	23,752,000
6.	GeoCities	21,303,000
7.	Excite Network	18,861,000
8.	Time Warner	13,257,000
9.	Blue Mountain Arts	11,089,000
10.	Amazon.com	10,736,000
11.	AltaVista Search	10,458,000
12.	Snap.com	9,761,000
13.	Xoom.com sites	9,693,000
14.	ZDNet Sites	9,043,000
15.	RealSite Portfolios	8,910,000
16.	Broadcast.com	8,593,000
17.	Juno	8,322,000
18.	Cnet	8,184,000
19.	EBay	8,083,000
20.	Infospace Impressions	7,653,000

Echo-boomers are a big, brand-conscious future market

This group of youthful consumers has been bombarded by brand messages in a multitude of media since the day they were born. They can't help but be brand-conscious, but they behave in ways that may confuse

Smart quotes

and disrupt traditional thinkers about brand management. Old-style slogan advertising worked well with prior generations, but not so well with this one. They are too smart, too hip, and too jaded to be hooked by just a catchy slogan. Instead, they respond to humor seasoned with irony and (gasp) topped off with a dose of the unvarnished truth!

Why is this so? It is hard to say for sure, but several factors come to mind. This is a well-informed, and incredibly diverse group, racially, ethnically, socially and economically. They see an incredible variety of messages on all kinds of media – cable TV, the Internet, ads in the movies, magazines, celebrity spokespersons, snowboarding tournament banners, and on and on. While many advertisers build their brands with this group via traditional network TV, their medium of choice is probably the Internet. Web-page design and branding of Internet products and services may turn out to be the ideal way to get to these echo-boomers, sometimes known as Generation Y or the Net generation – for good reason. The only generation who will have their lives more saturated than this one is the one following them – the "Net kids."

KILLER QUESTIONS

Are we speaking to all of the target audiences in languages they know, understand and prefer?

Kids will be important brand buyers of the future

Nearly 30% of the kids surveyed by Jupiter Communications in 1998 said they are watching less TV because they are online more of the time. Children's web sites like www.icanbuy.com are making it increasingly convenient for parents to authorize kids to shop on the web. This will make children's brands far more important as part of web commerce. Getting kids to buy on-line is tricky and many regulations forbid collecting information from them, but the size of the opportunity will motivate brand managers to find ways around these obstacles.

Kids and teens get around $75 per week to spend from sources such as gifts, allowances, and "pay" for chores around the house. This "income" represents a very large purchase segment that may be most easily and effectively tapped by brand managers via the web. This web based brand building must be done with care, because there is a risk of damaging a brand by an improper or tasteless web presence.

Smart
answers to
tough
questions

Q: How big is the teen market, and in what products?
A: Bigger than you thought.

Teen Piggy Banks (age 13–19)

Category	%	$Billion
Apparel	34%	$36.7
Entertainment	23.4%	$23.4
Food	15%	$16.7
Personal Care	9%	$9.2
Sporting Goods	6%	$6.7
Other	14%	$15.3

Total spending in 1996 = $108 Billion
Packaged Facts (InterRep Research)

One thing is sure in business – young people will get older, and the habits they learn young will grow up with them. This is why the habits of kids and teens is so important to brand managers of the future. According to Teenage Research Unlimited, a Chicago market research firm, 81% of teens use the web already, and the percentage can only increase further. Kids use it for a myriad of reasons from school research to playing games. They use it to download photos, read about their favorite stars, and they use it to shop! This is the brand manager's dream and nightmare all in one.

KILLER QUESTIONS

The old measure of CPM (cost per thousand impressions of an ad) is still valid, but are the impressions all of equal value?

The old rules are just no longer valid. It is so easy for anyone to put up a web site, and "go into business," that barriers to entry have fallen by the wayside. With this proliferation of sources, advertising becomes hugely different. Once there were three major TV networks. Now there are literally dozens of cable stations, and

Q: How big is the kids market? And for what kind of stuff?
A: Big and growing …

Kids Piggy Bank (age 4-12)

Category	%	$Billion
Food & Beverages	33%	$7.7
Toys, Games, etc.	28%	$6.5
Apparel	15%	$3.6
Movies/sports	8%	$2.0
Video Arcade, etc.	6%	$1.4
Other	10%	$2.2

Total spending in 1997=$23.4 Billion
Texas A&M, US Census Bureau

Smart answers to tough questions

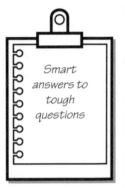

Q: Is the web really a meaningful advertising medium?
A: In dollars, not yet; but in growth it is likely to be one in the very near future!

Company	'98 Ad Revenues	'98 Sales & Mktg Exp. ($US million)
Yahoo (portal)	203	92
Excite (portal)	154	80
CNET (news)	49	15
SportsLineUSA (news)	18	21
Marketwatch.com (news)	5	12
Ivillage (women info)	9	20
TheStreet.com (news)	3	9
MapQuest (maps)	1	5
MiningCo.com (community)	2	3

more burgeoning new networks. With this enormous number of choices and adding the millions of web sites, brand advertising becomes a whole new proposition. The economics of promoting a brand become much more complex. Targeting becomes either much easier or much tougher, depending on the product, service and customer targets for the brand.

The chart above shows just the tip of the iceberg in advertising and sales/marketing expenses on the Internet. This kind of information shows the fragmentation and unusual spending patterns driven by web usage and the "give it away to get people to come see it."

Brand based communities on the web

One of the most intriguing opportunities for brands on the Internet is to build them via web communities. Building communities of purchasers has often been prohibitively expensive in the past, because it was geographically limited. The global reach and targeting precision of web based marketing makes building these selected communities both easier and more attractive.

When a group of like-minded consumers are physically distributed around a country, a continent or the world, reaching them with a brand message via conventional geographically based media is impractical if not impossible. The web knows no geographical boundaries and thus it can aggregate this community of customers into a large enough group to make brand-building both practical and potentially lucrative. This kind of new aggregation of brand buyers can be an important part of branding in the future.

My measure is better than your measure

One of the challenges you will face when promoting brands on the Internet is knowing exactly what results you got and what value you received. Measures of web-based activity comprise a plethora of competing and often conflicting claims. You'll have to decide what and who to believe. Take the example of online magazine, *Salon.* The Salon web site claimed that 1.2 million people visited the site in February of 1999. Media Metrix, the best known of the Internet ratings agencies says fewer than 500,000. That is a huge difference. How would an aspiring brand manager decide on the effectiveness, reach and frequency or even approximate the CPM (cost per thousand impressions) for brand promotion/advertising when such radically different statistics exist?

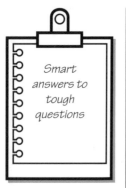

Q: Can you believe Web Statistics?
A: Nobody knows yet. They may only be directionally accurate.

How the Unique Visitor Count varies: what is the Truth??

Site	Host	MediaMetrix	Neilsen
MapQuest	3,975	2,742	1,800
The NY Times	2,124	1,841	1,090
The Onion	1,800	405	184
Cars.com	1,182	674	504
Slate	446	411	173

There is not yet any widely accepted standard measure of web site activity – qualitatively. Counters may register "hits," but do those hits mean anything? Some sites and statistic gatherers count unique visitors, but even that definition is perilously fuzzy. Examples of further confusion are in the table above.

A quick glance at the variation in the statistics in the table above reveals how risky reliance on advertising reach and CPM can be. Who do you believe? Media Metrix has a panel of 40,000 people responding, but critics complain that it is skewed because only 5000 are users at work. Media Metrix cautions that their sample is constantly evolving to represent the best possible cross-section of people using the web. Neilsen only measures 14,000 users and concedes it must increase its base significantly. Where do the site hosts get their numbers? Who knows. Perhaps from a simple counter that measures hits but gives no qualitative data.

When are there too many brands to sort out?

You will have to deal with brand proliferation that creates problems of too many names competing for space in the time-starved consumer's consciousness. Worse yet, those brands, including yours, are competing across a huge number of media channels; more than ever before and increasing with astronomical speed. The dilemma is made worse by brand extensions and sub-brands. Kraft has dozens of varieties of cheese and cheese-like products. Oscar Mayer has a similar range of packaged luncheon meats. At least 20–50 distinct types of bread are displayed in a typical supermarket. The simple decision of how to buy the ingredients for a sandwich might present 250,000 options of just these three ingredients and the associated condiments – mustard (regular, Dijon style, with horseradish, etc.), ketchup, pickles, mayonnaise, relish, and so forth.

Brands must break through this clutter – but how? One way is to be different. Miracle Whip sandwich spread/salad dressing has succeeded, but there are few that compare to its success at presenting itself as a desirable alternative to mayonnaise. Picante sauce now outsells ketchup (or catsup), almost entirely due to marketing of it as a desirable, low-fat, tangy, chip dip and condiment. Pace brand sells itself as different in advertising by portraying itself as originating in an area where Picante sauce and Hispanic population are more prevalent – a clever positioning in a crowded field.

Smart quotes

> You can't use old measures like reach and frequency. It's not about how many eyeballs you get. You have to be sure your buy is very targeted. If you want to sell hamburgers, you don't want broad reach. You want hamburger eaters, and you want them every day. On the Internet, reach is not as key as continuity.
>
> Sergio Zyman, *The End Of Marketing As We Know It*, cited in *Business Week*, June 7, 1999, p.59

The "adjacent-possibles" increase and the niches get narrower

Retailing is a good example of how proliferation creates opportunities and risks. The US is over-retailed by at least one third. Management Horizons, the Columbus OH-based research firm, and Dr Roger Blackwell, noted consumer-behavior expert, both cite this over-stored condition regularly. For each new store that opens, at least one must close – go out of business. Niches get narrower and narrower, or stores get broader and broader. Wal*Mart, Kmart, Target, Meijer Carrefour and Fred Meyer all are opening more and more 150,000-square-foot superstores which contain at least a general merchandise discount store a full supermarket complete with deli and bakery, a pharmacy, and other specialty services like film processing, eyeglass exams and sales, etc. One stop does it almost completely, but a quick stop is almost impossible due to the store and parking-lot size and distances involved. This type of retailing trend has continued to spread in Europe too.

The alternative is the neighborhood store, the convenient store, gas station, and coffee stop, which are found on the street corners of every major intersection and freeway interchange. One stop does only a little, but these stores are studies in focused merchandising of frequently needed items (like gas, cigarettes, bread and milk) or impulse items like junk food and lottery tickets. Brands must gain the shopper's attention instantly, or be

Smart quotes

Brand is a virtual experience derived from the consumer's experiences with product, service, or company – not from messages of broadcast media. The development of brand requires that an infrastructure of distribution, support and service be in place when and where the consumer wants it. Real-time technology delivers the brand experience any time, any place.

Regis McKenna, *Real Time* (Harvard Business School Press, 1997)

already in the shopper's mind when they stop. Advertisers and merchandisers of cigarettes and soft drinks sell to this niche aggressively.

Home Depot stores are the superstore of the home improvement and building industry in the US. This retailer has become so powerful and so trusted that they are beginning to create and segment markets with their own captive brands. By combining major brands of products and crossing categories with them, they can own not only the brand but also the right to use it. You can find a lawn tractor made by John Deere, carrying the Scotts brand and sold exclusively at Home Depot. In this case the retailer becomes the brand manager, but for other people's brands. Dangerous for the brands' integrity? Yes! Powerful for sales? You bet!

At the other end of the spectrum, go to the local mall or airport. Kiosks and carts line the centers of the concourses with niche items from Beanie Babies to baseball caps. Stores specializing in sunglasses or candles are sure to be there. The niches are so small that different carts of kiosks sell costume jewelry located only fifty feet from one selling real gold jewelry in glass counters, which is just across the aisle from a full service jewelry store with gems, gold and sizing services. Elsewhere in the mall, Gucci or Tiffany sell the cachet of their unique brand – all at the super premium prices of a prestige brand.

Smart quotes

New media and technologies like multi-media, the Internet, and virtual reality provide immense opportunities for grabbing customers and providing them with satisfying combinations of text, pictures, and videos as well as sound touch and smell ... For all these reasons, the branding phase is losing its vitality and being replaced by the marketing of sensory experiences.

Bernd Schmitt & Alex Simonson

PCs surpass TVs in sales in the US! What are the implications of this statistic on brands and branding? One certainly is that you'd better understand the world as seen by PC users and web surfers, or you are looking at less than the entire picture of the brand world. Brands will never be the same again. Since 1995, the web has exploded in a growth curve so steep, that only the most brazen forecasters have even been aggressive enough with their estimates of user growth and user count. The hours spent on the Internet can only increase further. Is your brand there? When will it be? How effectively will it be presented. This is a large part of any brand builder's job in the coming century.

Leaders must breed their own revolutionaries, and then listen to them

An established fact is that industry leaders never develop the technology and ideas that prove to be their demise. They are too invested in what they are doing as leaders to knock themselves off. Someone else always does it – and leaves the old leader scrambling to recover. So, if you and your company are successful leaders now, you are in great danger!

SMART VOICES

Steve Goubeaux of VMA states that he believes the greatest challenge faced by brand managers and creative marketers of today's business environment is addressing the generation differences between marketers and consumers especially with the rapid rate of change – especially with the younger generations. In his words, "The older people (in their 30s and 40s) who are usually making or approving the marketing and advertising plans often don't have a clue how to talk to the Generation Y kids in their teens and the younger generation overall."

Product or service concepts become popular and then disappear so rapidly, that anyone who is not really connected to the youth and their whims and wishes will always be too late or out of fashion. Clear positioning is incredibly important during this blizzard of new brands. Without such focused brand positions, blurring of brand meanings will inevitably occur. When this happens, confused consumers buy other, more clearly focused brands.

KILLER QUESTIONS

What are the greatest risks to our brand, and if we were to attack ourselves, how would we do it? What would we do if a competitor attacked us that way?

One solution that has worked in some situations is to create an internal "Generation Group of Brand Revolutionaries." This is a separate, protected cell of free thinking, much younger people who are more rebellious, more aggressive, far less encumbered by policies, protocol and past practices and in touch with today's trends and fads. Commission them to "knock off" the parent corporation's brand positions and support them while they try. Use everything you know about your weaknesses to help them, but tie them to the company with recognition, and rewards (e.g. stock deals) so strong that their being stolen by competitors is virtually impossible. Then watch carefully what they come up with. Put one of the most forward thinking, aggressive, and respected (younger) brand managers/leaders in charge, and make sure he/she stays out of their way as much as possible.

If this group succeeds in coming up with a brand or marketing strategy that could really hurt in the hands of a competitor, be thankful that it was done internally. Then enlist their help in figuring out how to combat it, if a competitor comes up with something similar. The key is to figure out how to hold onto the new leadership position by using the right parts of the old knowledge and the right parts of the new knowledge. If you don't, someone else will! That is the one certainty in the future of brands and branding. Nothing lives forever, but some things live a lot longer than others – make sure that your career, your business and your brand will be one of those.

Index